AF496438

PICASSO

PICASSO

O. B. DUANE

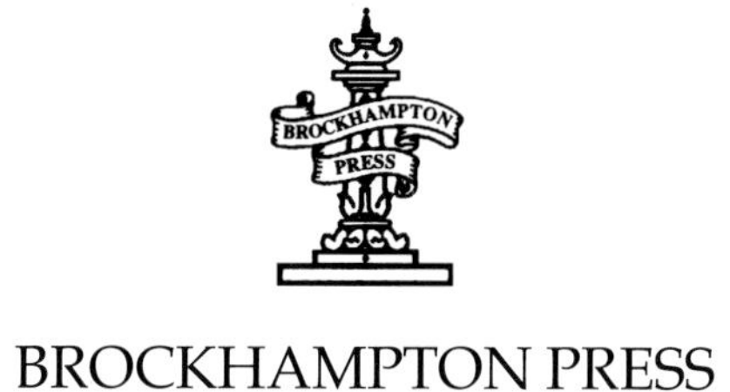

BROCKHAMPTON PRESS

First published in Great Britain by Brockhampton Press,
a member of the Hodder Headline Group,
20 Bloomsbury Street, London WC1B 3QA

ISBN 1 86019 150 9

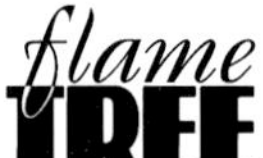

Produced by Flame Tree Publishing,
The Long House, Antrobus Road, Chiswick, London W4 5HY
for Brockhampton Press
A Wells/McCreeth/Sullivan Production

Pictures printed courtesy of the Visual Arts Library, London,
and Edimedia, Paris, and with thanks to the Picasso Estate.

Printed and bound by Oriental Press, Dubai

CONTENTS

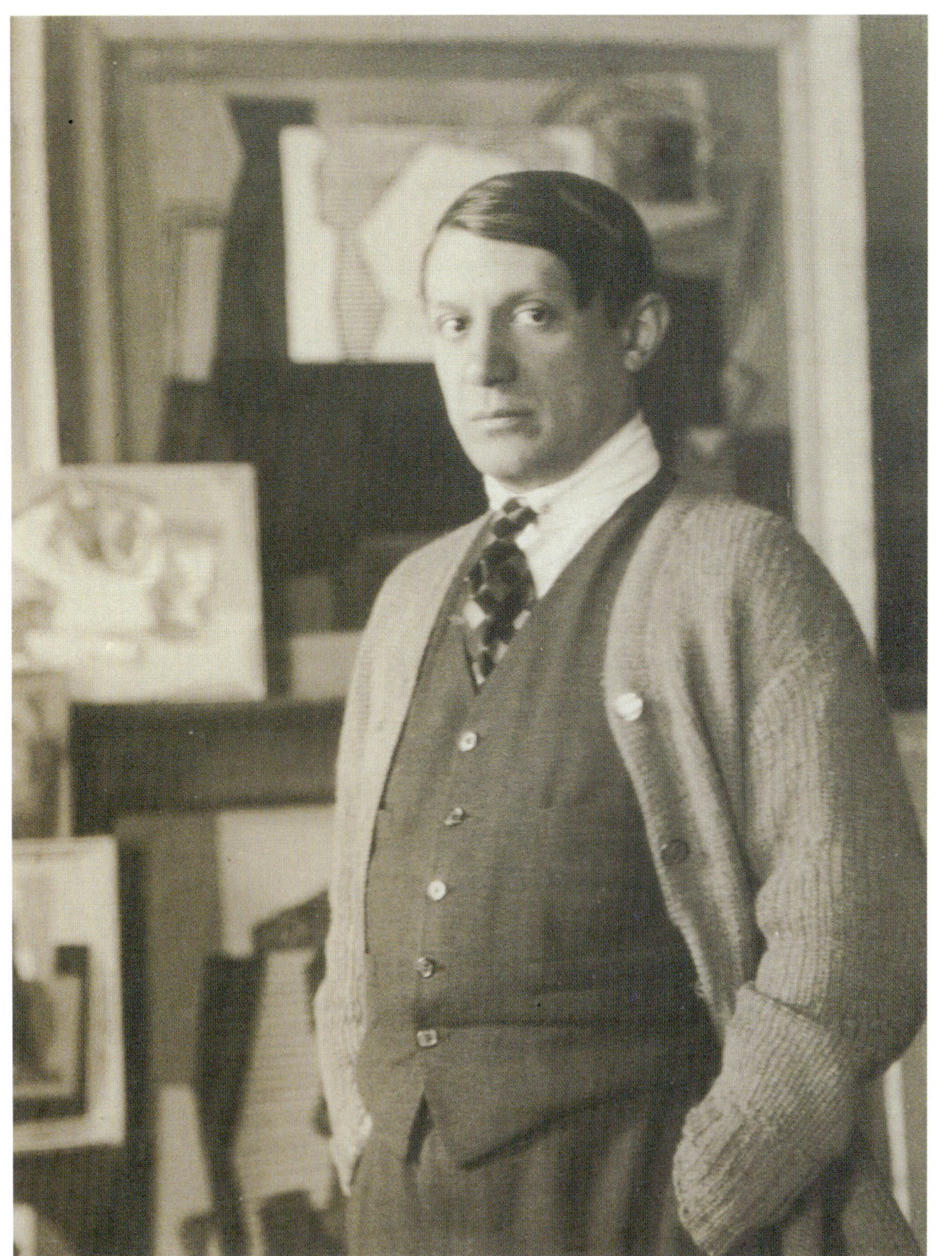

Picasso, 1923 (Philadelphia Museum of Art) Picasso was a strikingly good-looking man with a highly charismatic, yet often difficult personality. Man Ray took this photograph of him in 1923, when the artist was forty-two years old.

CHRONOLOGY

1881	Picasso born on 25 October in the city of Malaga, on Spain's southern coast.
1890	Paints first oil painting, entitled *Picador,* when he is nine years old.
1891	Family moves from Malaga to La Coruna on the north-west Atlantic coast.
1895	Family moves again to Barcelona.
1896	Picasso's work exhibited alongside Barcelona's most prominent artists of the day, Santiago Rusinol and Isidre Nonell.
1897	*Science and Charity* receives critical acclaim at the National Exhibition of Fine Arts in Madrid. Picasso attends the Royal Academy of San Fernando.
1900	Picasso journeys to Paris for the first time with fellow artist, Carlos Casagemas. He paints *Le Moulin de la Galette* and *The Embrace.*
1901	Picasso enters his 'Blue Period', prompted by the suicide of Casagemas. He paints *Evocation – The Burial of Casagemas, The Blue Room, Child with a Pigeon, Le Bock* and a particularly stark self-portrait at this time.
1903	He returns to Barcelona and remains here for over a year, painting the best of his 'Blue Period' works, including *La Vie* and *Les Pauvres au Bord de la Mer.*
1904	Picasso returns to Paris to settle there permanently. Moves to the Bateau Lavoir and completes *The Frugal Repast.* Meets Fernande Olivier.
1905	The start of Picasso's 'Rose Period'.
1906	Picasso meets two important collectors, Gertrude Stein and Wilhelm Uhde. He paints Gertrude's portrait. Travels to Gosol for his summer holiday.
1907	*Les Demoiselles d'Avignon*, Picasso's first Cubist painting, is completed.
1908	Picasso begins to collaborate with the Frenchman, Georges Braque, and Cubism is born.
1911	While on holiday in Céret with Braque, Picasso develops a 'collage' technique; Synthetic Cubism evolves.
1914	The First World War ends Picasso's partnership with Braque. Picasso begins to journey away from Cubism towards a Neoclassical style.
1916	Picasso meets the composer, Eric Satie.
1917	Picasso travels to Rome to work on the ballet, *Parade*, with Satie. Meets his future wife Olga Khokhlova.
1918	Marries Olga in Paris in July.
1921	Picasso paints two large canvases, *Three Musicians*, his last great Cubist paintings. His son, Paolo is born in February.
1925	*The Three Dancers* is chosen to illustrate Surrealist ideology. *Les Demoiselles d'Avignon* is reproduced for the first time in a Surrealist magazine.
1927	Picasso meets the seventeen-year-old, Marie-Thérèse Walter.
1929	Picasso begins his most intense period of sculpture in collaboration with Julio Gonzalez.
1934	Begins a series of etchings, *The Sculptor's Studio*, in honour of Marie-Thérèse.
1935	Marie-Thérèse gives birth to a daughter, Maya. Picasso separates from Olga. Produces etching: *Minotauromachie.*
1936	Civil war erupts in Spain.
1937	*The Dream and Lie of Franco*, a series of engravings completed. Guernica bombed by Franco. Picasso begins *Guernica Frieze*. Meets Dora Maar. Paints *Weeping Woman.*
1939	Picasso refuses to leave Paris despite the outbreak of the Second World War.
1942	Paints *Still-Life with Steer's Skull.*
1944	Paints *Charnel House* in response to the Nazi concentration camp atrocities. Exhibits at the Autumn Salon in Paris. Joins the French Communist Party.
1945	Meets Françoise Gilot.
1947	Françoise gives birth to Picasso's son, Claude.
1948	Paloma Picasso is born, Picasso's fourth child.
1949	Picasso creates a lithograph of a Milanese pigeon which is used by the French Communist Party to announce their World Congress.
1952	Picasso meets Jacqueline Roque.
1953	Françoise Gilot leaves Picasso.
1955	Death of Olga Khokhlova. Picasso moves to Cannes with Jacqueline Roque.
1957	Picasso begins a series of variations on Velázquez' *Las Meninas.*
1961	Paints his version of Manet's *Le Déjeuner sur l'Herbe*. Marries for the second time at the age of eighty. Moves near to Mougins.
1966	Giant retrospective show held in Paris to celebrate Picasso's eighty-fifth birthday.
1968	Death of Sabartés. Picasso donates *Las Meninas* series to Barcelona Picasso museum.
1973	Picasso dies at the age of ninety-two.

*Two Brothers***, 1906 (Musée Picasso, Paris)** During his Rose Period, Picasso introduced new subject matter, illuminated by warm pink tones, and concentrated on perfecting his drawing technique. This painting has none of the morbid atmosphere of his Blue Period.

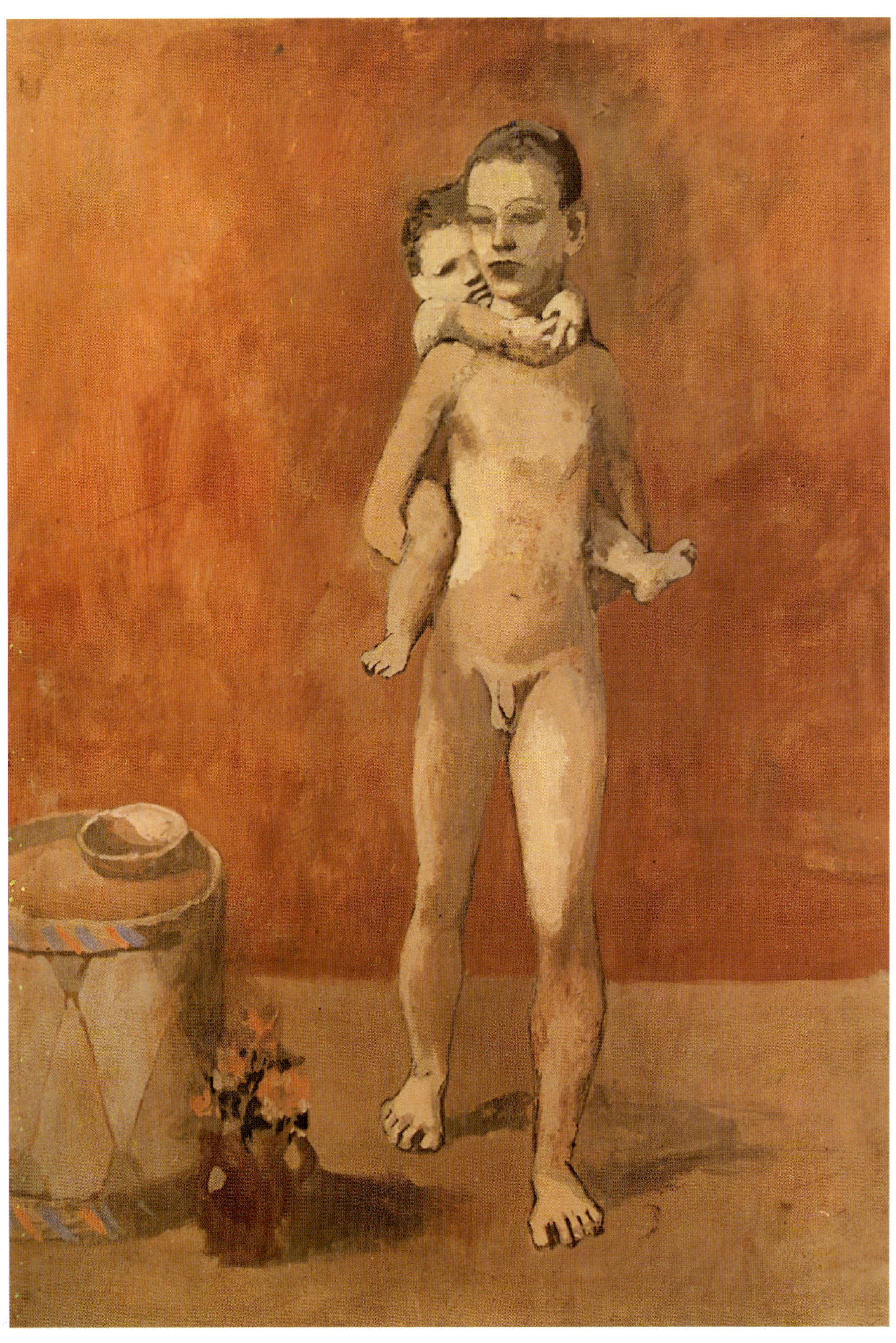

CHAPTER 1

From Prodigy to Rebel (1881-1901)

To this day, Picasso is remembered as a 'genius', a truly exhaustive artistic talent whose impact on twentieth-century art defies all measurement.

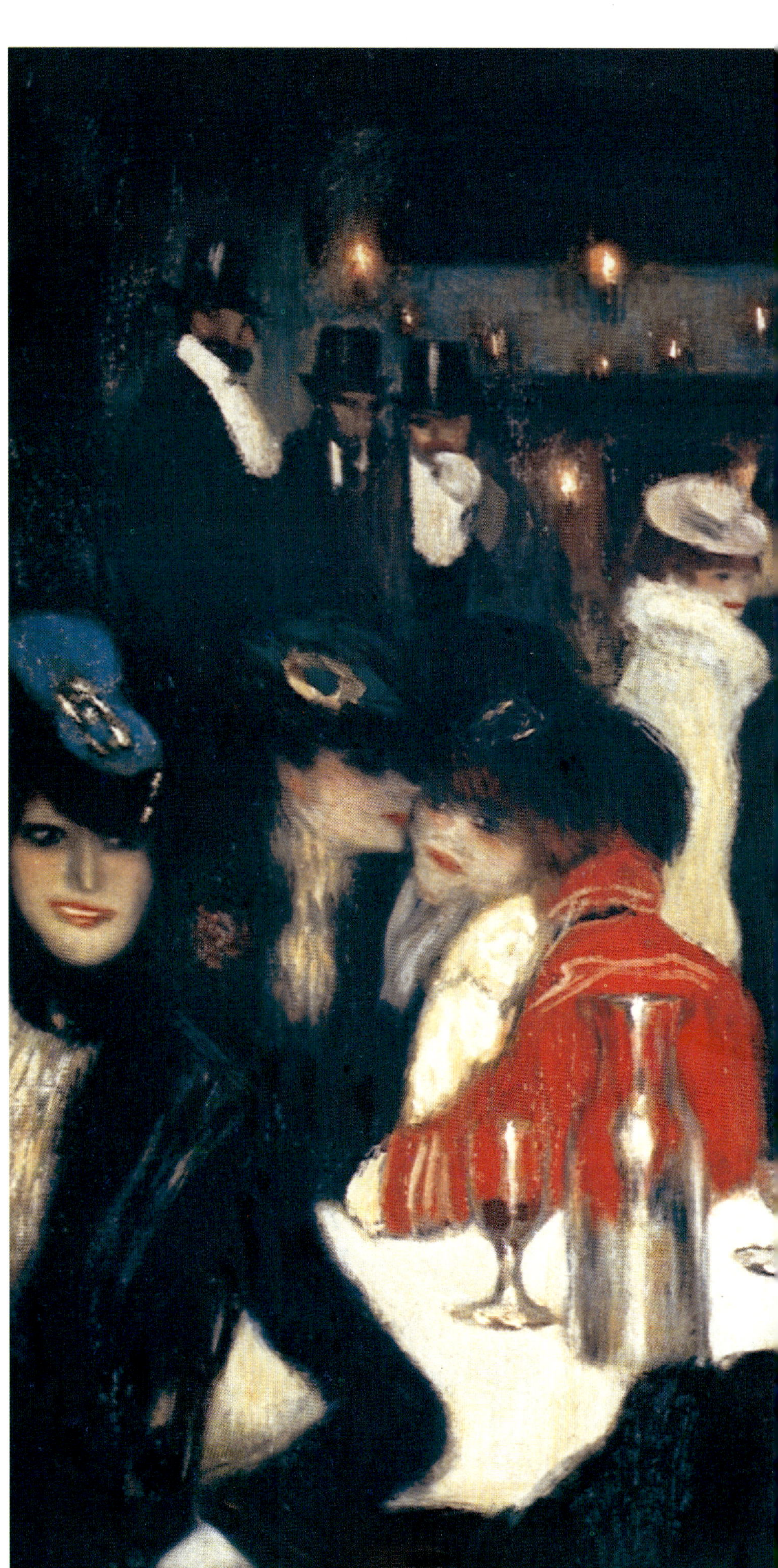

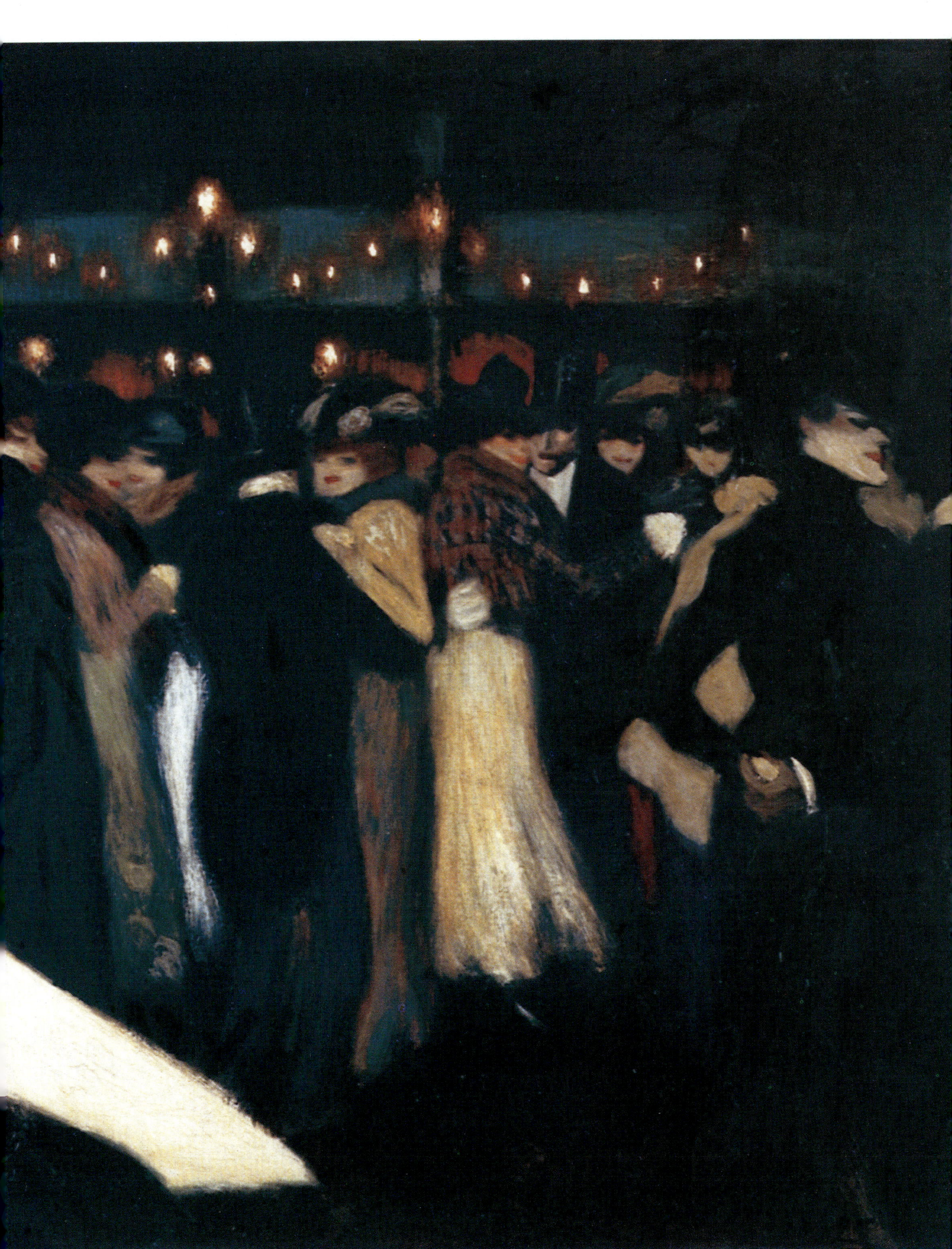

Art critics, scholars, journalists and amateur enthusiasts have been saturated with evidence of Picasso's astonishing creativity over the course of a career which spanned almost eight decades. Not all of his work has met with the admiration of critics or the viewing public, yet his diversity, his unrelenting quest for variety, and extraordinary gift of invention, bear witness to the fact that his importance to the world of art can never be over-stated.

Picasso's immense output was to extend across most modern art movements. He journeyed through the Blue, Rose, Cubist, classical, Surrealist and tragic movements of artistic expression, invariably at the forefront of any group seeking to introduce innovations or probe deeper into the fundamental role of the artist. He was to prove himself a multi-dimensional talent exploring, with equal fervour and success, the varied media of painting, drawing, engraving, sculpture and ceramics. His style, fired by a fiercely independent and restless spirit, changed path repeatedly and without warning, each new direction serving only to enhance his popularity and renew his impulse to invent yet further. There seems to have been no limit to Picasso's energy. Even in later life, his productivity did not diminish and he continued to paint until his death at the age of ninety-two. He remains perhaps the most prolific and innovative artist this century has ever known.

Pablo Ruiz Picasso was born in October 1881 in southern Spain, in the city of Malaga. He was born into a secure middle-class background, although the story of his birth purports an arrival into the world that was anything but secure. The midwife who delivered Pablo abandoned him for dead and it was his uncle who helped him establish a firmer presence, by blowing cigar smoke into his face, at which point Pablo remembered to exercise his lungs. Picasso is said to have inherited his coal-black hair and remarkable dark brown eyes from his mother, Maria Picasso Lopez, who was the daughter of a Malagan civil servant. Picasso's father, Don José Ruiz Blasco, worked as a museum curator, art teacher and painter of average ability. Pablo was an only son and he was doted on by his two sisters and mother. He received every encouragement from them at an early age to draw and paint. His sisters would challenge him to draw animals from a variety of starting points and by the age of five he displayed an amazing dexterity with a pencil. His father, in particular, had a profound influence on his early artistic development. Don José was keen to instruct his son and invited him to watch and learn while he painted landscape scenes and images of bull-fights or pigeons. The young Picasso soon immersed himself in the world of art. He would draw and sketch and began to assess his environment almost exclusively in terms of its visual appeal, reproducing subjects on paper that were most familiar to him – bull-fights, portraits of his sisters and parents, the birds which his father kept. He

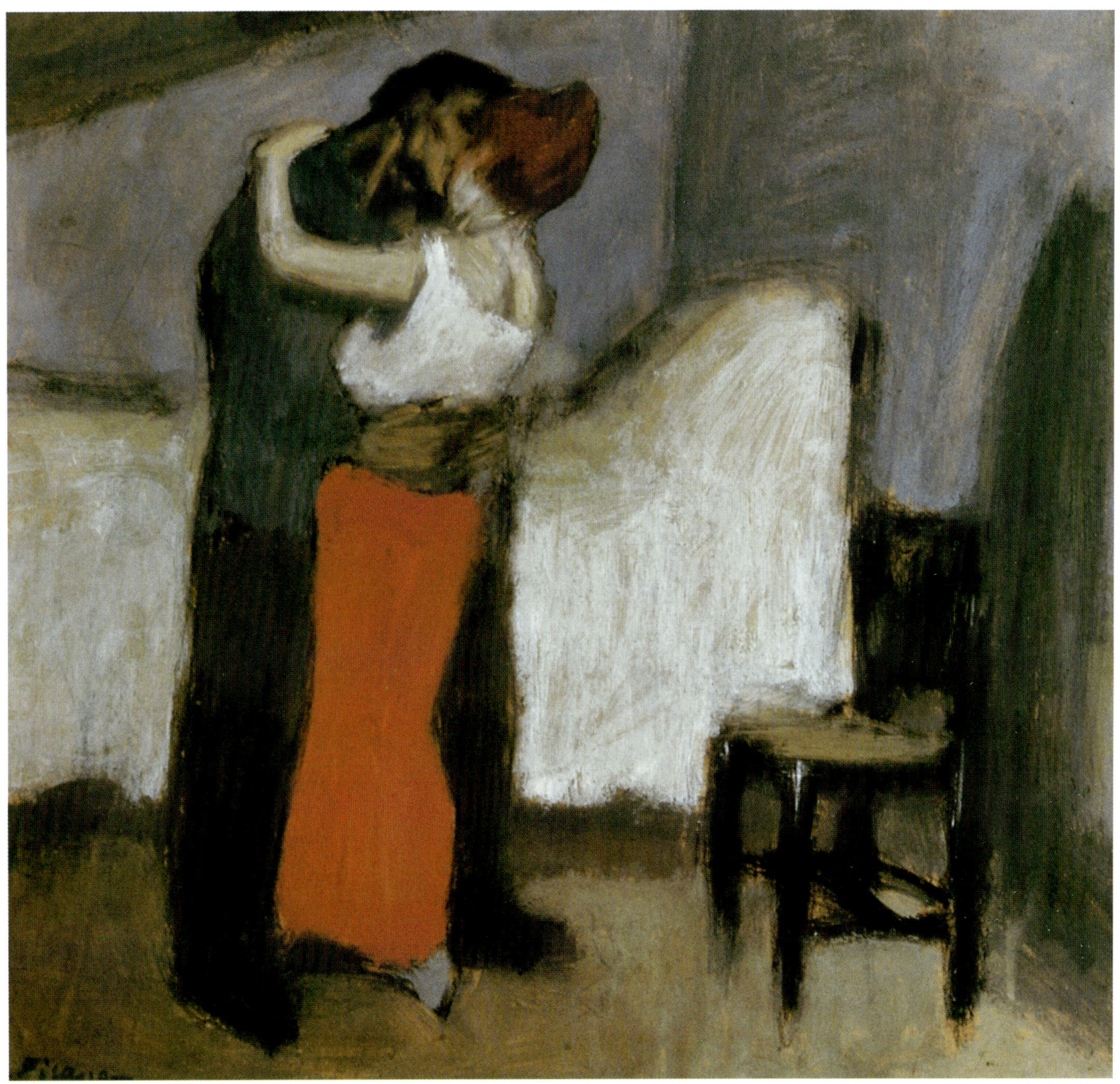

had no desire to go to school and could not understand the purpose of
any subject other than art. He displayed a terrifying independence at
an extremely young age, informing his parents that he would only
attend school if he could draw and paint there as much as he pleased.
He preferred to visit the bull-fights, which were to remain a passion
throughout his life, and they would be the subject of his first oil
entitled *Picador*, painted in 1890, when he was just nine years old.

The Ruiz family remained in Malaga for the first ten years of
Picasso's life. In 1891, the museum where Don José worked was forced
to close and the family moved to the north of Spain, to La Coruna, on

The Embrace, **1900 (Moscow, Pushkin
Museum)** Picasso was on the verge of
discovering his own unique style of the
Blue Period when he completed this
painting. He would soon abandon all
contrasts of colour within his work, in
favour of monochrome, reflecting a
mood of despair which gripped him for
the next four years.

Violin and Compote, **1913 (Philidelphia Museum of Art)** Picasso was exclusively committed to Cubism for a period of about about nine years from 1907. After this time, he began to allow other influences to penetrate his work. Still-life images were a particular favourite of Cubist artists and were most colourfully portrayed during the period of Synthetic Cubism, after 1911.

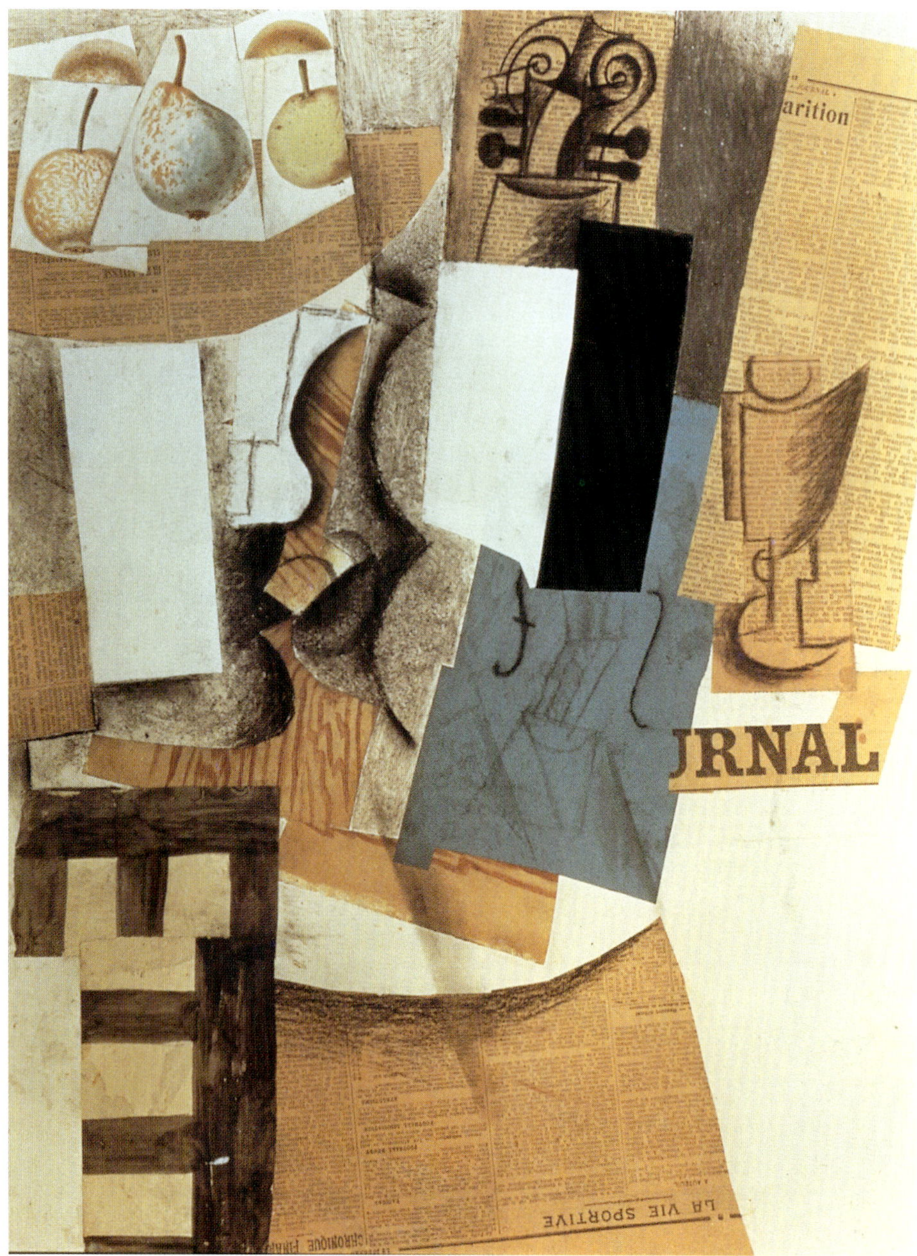

the Atlantic coast where they spent the next four years. Young Pablo's talent as an artist now began to blossom in earnest. Before he had reached the age of thirteen, he could draw like Raphael and had learned all that Don José could possibly teach him. Reflecting on this fact in later life, Picasso remarked that he never possessed the clumsiness of a seven year old with a pencil, but made academic drawings whose minute precision frightened him. It took many years for him to learn how to draw like a child.

While the young prodigy evidently answered all his father's hopes for him, Don José undoubtedly felt the shadow of his son gradually eclipse his own light. One day he asked Pablo to finish the feet of a pigeon he had been painting and, on seeing the result, was forced to admit that his son's talent far surpassed his own. As Picasso recalled it, 'he handed me his paint and his brush and never painted again'. After this time, Picasso no longer signed his works P. Ruiz, but adopted his mother's name, following a Spanish custom of linking maternal and paternal family names.

Picasso's father now focused his energies on ensuring that his son receive a sound academic education in art which he considered to be the only proper course forward. He encouraged Pablo to study and copy the old masters and to capture exact likenesses through a highly disciplined approach which left little room for imaginative exploration. Some of Picasso's earliest surviving works reflect this powerful influence. He painted a portrait of his sister Lola in December 1894 and drew his father's reclining figure in January 1895. Both works are breathtakingly mature, perfectly proportioned and realistically executed, affirming the fact that he had little difficulty coming to grips with the rigorously controlled style of classical art. A procession of subsequent works, including several portraits, such as *Barefoot Girl* and *Man in a Cap*, display a remarkable proficiency, yet also a desire to penetrate deeper into the souls of his models. Picasso was already beginning to struggle with the restraints of the classical techniques to which Don José adhered and attempted to instil in him. He had begun to seek out a less traditional, more individual style. His soul-searching journey was increasingly reflected in his work, eventually leading to an implacable division of opinion between himself and his father.

By 1895, when Picasso was fourteen, Don José was offered a prestigious teaching post at the 'La Lonja' art academy in Barcelona and the family moved to this city with its cosmopolitan population and colourful Mediterranean atmosphere in the autumn of that year. Pablo had begun to outgrow the provincialism of La Coruna and welcomed this widening of his world. His father arranged for him to attend the academy, but this proved only a reminder of the things he sought to escape. Pablo could not take any of his art classes seriously, an attitude which was not helped by the fact that the exam pieces he submitted to qualify for a place proved to be of a higher standard that the work of most senior students at the school. Don José knew that his prodigy son would need careful monitoring if he was to avoid boredom, or worse still, fall victim to the decadent influences of modernist ideas. His father rented him a studio in the Calle de la Plata and it was here in 1896 that Picasso painted *First Communion* and *Science and Charity*, both projects carefully supervised by Don José, satisfying all academic standards of realism and nostalgia. At fifteen, Picasso had earned the respect of the most distinguished artists in Barcelona and exhibited his early work in 1896, alongside two of the city's most prominent figures, Santiago Rusinol and Isidre Nonell. The canvas *Science and Charity*, depicting a bed-ridden woman attended by a doctor and a nun, also

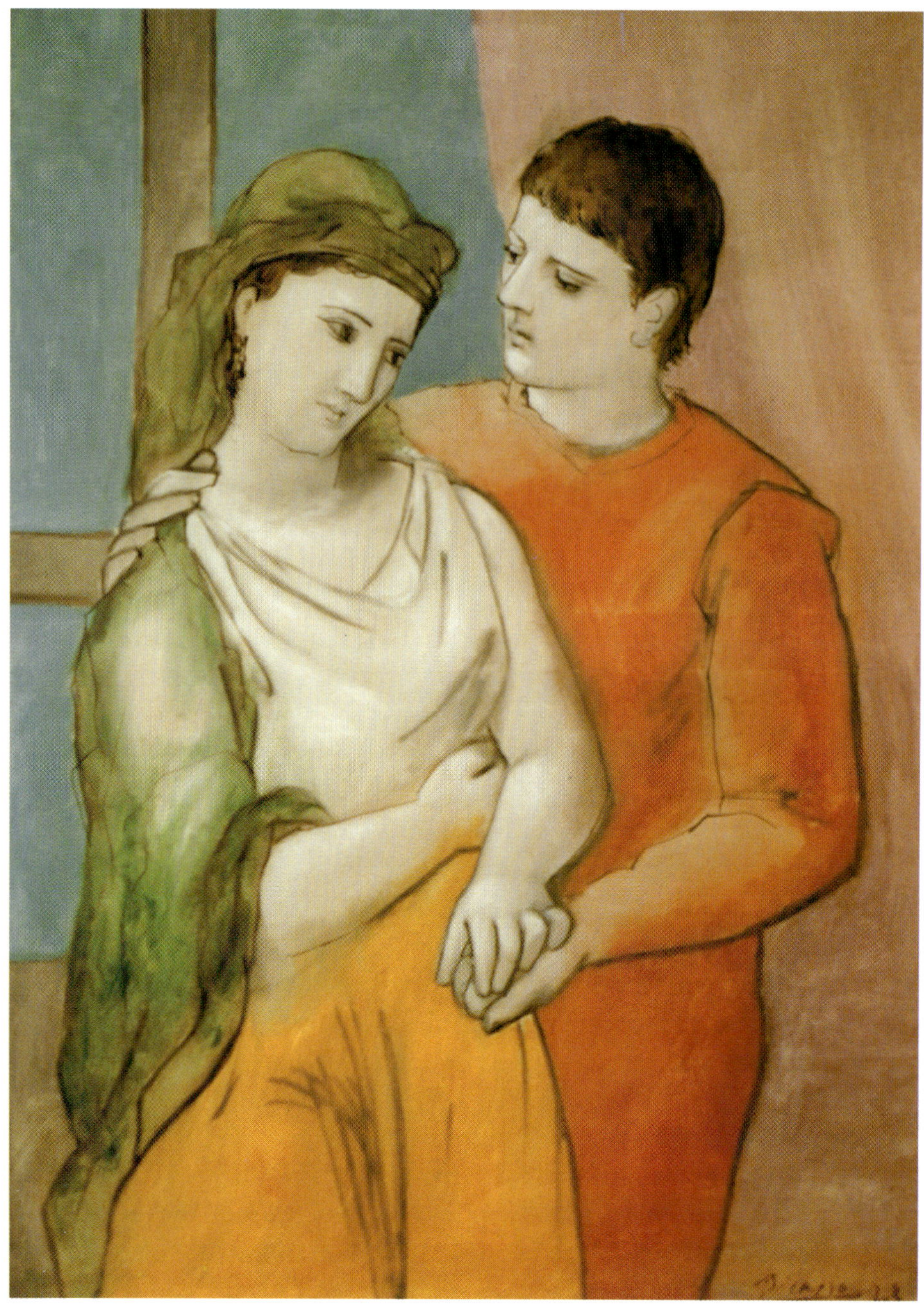

***Les Amants*, 1936 (Private Collection)**
Picasso could readily adapt to any style of painting. His father had instilled in him an appreciation of classical art from a very early age and it was a style of painting he returned to frequently, adding his own idiosyncratic touches.

won him a highly favourable reception at the National Exhibition of Fine Arts in Madrid in 1897.

Having decided that his son needed more invigorating instruction than the 'La Lonja' academy could provide, Don José arranged for Pablo to attend the Royal Academy of San Fernando in Madrid, the most respected school for artists in Spain. Picasso's independent streak refused to be suppressed however, and within a few weeks of arriving in the city, he had stopped attending classes. He could no longer tolerate the academic pedantry and formal structure of art establishments and spent his time wandering the city looking for fresh themes and inspiration for paintings of his own. He frequently visited the Prado

Museum, which housed magnificent collections of paintings by Goya and Velázquez, among others. He also became passionately interested in the works of El Greco, in the unique and unorthodox style of this sixteenth-century Spanish painter. El Greco's elongated figures and unusual colouring had made him an unpopular Spanish artist, but Picasso was entranced by his work, instinctively responding to the intense and passionate involvement the artist had with his subject, needing to experience that same unprecedented freedom in his own creations.

He began to send drawings home to his father which reflected the influence of El Greco, an anti-realism had crept into his work and he now sketched elongated limbs and eccentric, mystical faces, favouring spontaneity of creation, rather than a studied approach. This disregard for his classical training deeply disappointed Don José. He wrote to his son, dismissing his drawings, stating that Picasso was intent on 'following the bad way'. His father's approval and guidance mattered little now and Picasso's spirit of independence drove him to flout tradition, to fight with his art like a true revolutionary. Although little of Picasso's work from this period survives, the painting *Tavern Interior* foreshadows his future artistic course. Its departure from the use of posed subjects and its emphasis on heavy brushwork and dark colours confirm that the young artist was gradually passing from acceptance to refusal. He was all the time creating challenges for himself, plunging deeper and deeper into a knowledge of the world and of people, so that this knowledge might liberate him little by little.

Picasso stopped attending the San Fernando Academy in Madrid when he contracted scarlet fever in the spring of 1898. He never again returned there for tuition. He left the city and journeyed to the remote Pyrénées village of Horta de Ebro with a friend, Manuel Pallares, to recuperate from his illness over the next eight months. The visit to the tiny village had a dramatic effect on his art. 'I learnt everything I know in Pallares' village,' Picasso pronounced many years later, for it was here that he came face to face with the simple life of peasants and gained both a sense of compassion and a new confidence in his work, divorced from the influences of the academy and of his family. In early 1899, he returned to Barcelona, burning with new ideas and full of ambitious plans. He was only eighteen years old, but he had partly satisfied the search for his own self. He was remarkably immune to the dominance of others and was determined to pursue the life of an artist entirely on his own terms. He refused to re-enrol at 'La Lonja' where his father was still teaching but set out instead to take advantage of everything the city of Barcelona had to offer.

By the end of the nineteenth century Barcelona, not unlike Paris, had earned itself something of a reputation as a breeding ground for progressive modernist philosophies and concepts of art. The city

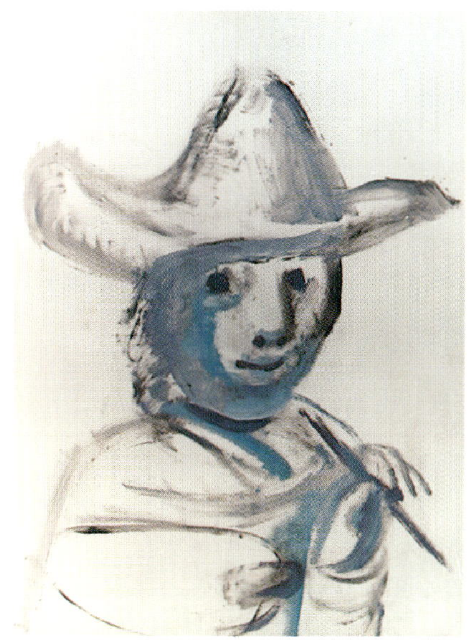

The Young Painter, 1972 (**Musée Picasso, Paris**) The remarkable simplicity of this painting has an effect equally powerful to any of Picasso's highly complex pieces.

provided a cross-roads for all European innovations originating not only in Paris, but in England, Vienna and also Munich. Nietzsche, Ibsen, the Pre-Raphaelites, William Morris, Maeterlinck and *art nouveau* were some of the familiar subjects of discussion at the headquarters of the Spanish avant-garde artists, an inn known as Els Quatre Gats, the 'Four Cats'. Picasso was soon a regular visitor and met here with all manner of artists, writers and sculptors, among them Isidre Nonell, Julio Gonzalez, Jaime Sabartés, Carlos Casagemas, Ramon Casas, Santiago Rusinol and Miguel Utrillo. His youth did not hinder him in any way and he was soon comfortable in the company of these prominent men, imitating their art, arguing his opinion, absorbing their wisdom and very rapidly emulating them in all that they had achieved. Picasso earned the deep respect of these older artists and was invited to give the first exhibition of his work, much of it consisting of portraits of his artist friends, in the tiny gallery attached to the pub. He had cultivated and perfected a 'Greco' style of painting, favouring long, sweeping strokes and bold colours. By 1900, he had moved out of his family home, broken free of his classical education, received his first important reviews and developed an increasingly decisive individual style.

Paris beckoned and its appeal could no longer be ignored. The city which had nurtured Chéret, Toulouse-Lautrec, Degas and Renoir continued to attract a disproportionate share of fresh artistic talent. Picasso travelled to Paris with his friend and fellow painter Carlos Casagemas in 1900, arriving in time to share in the feverish excitement of the Great Exhibition where the works of many of the masters he admired were being displayed. *Art nouveau* had taken centre stage, but the works of the Impressionists were also officially exhibited for the very first time. Picasso was inspired by artists like Manet and Degas and strove to follow their example in challenging Renaissance conventions in art, which they had replaced with a personal vision of everyday reality. Manet had shocked the art world by painting a nude in an ordinary, unromantic setting in 1863. His *Le Déjeuner sur l'herbe*, did not depict woman as Venus, as Raphael had done, but as a modern, fleshy female. Post-Impressionists, like Cézanne, Van Gogh and Gauguin, who considered the emotions of the artist equally, if not more, important to the material surroundings portrayed, had an especially profound impact on Picasso. Cubism, which Picasso went on to develop with Georges Braque, owed a particular debt to Cézanne who introduced a new concept of form in his painting, transforming objects beyond an accepted appearance, allowing them an internal life, free of the restraints of academic composition.

Picasso settled with Casagemas in a little studio in the Montmartre region of the city, a dilapidated area which had been the centre of bloody anarchist violence during the Paris Commune of the

1890s. Although it housed many of the city's Bohemian artists, Montmartre was also crowded with prostitutes, pimps, petty criminals, tramps, circus performers, and lowlife of every nationality, conveniently overlooked by Paris' *belle époque* culture. In spite of the poverty of his conditions, Picasso was determined to prove his ability in the world's largest arena of art. He allowed the influences around him to seep into his work. He frequently visited the Louvre and the Musée du Luxembourg and turned to the Paris streets for his subject matter. He brightened his palette and assimilated the techniques of the great works he had seen at first hand. His best surviving painting of this period, *Le Moulin de la Galette*, is obviously inspired by Lautrec and Degas. It is based on Renoir's original, painted in 1876, but does not reflect the gaiety and abandon of Renoir's work. Picasso's subjects are not depicted happily waltzing in daylight, in subdued tones evoking an atmosphere of gentle summer. He reproduces instead the more luminous shades of Toulouse-Lautrec and opts for a simplified modelling of his figures, imitating the softer outlines of Degas.

During this first stay in Paris, Picasso painted regularly. He painted café scenes, night-life, street perspectives, dances and horse races. He met Pedro Manyac at this time, a young gallery curator who greatly admired his work. Manyac became Picasso's first patron and his regular payments of 150 francs in exchange for a contract to produce a few paintings per month enabled Picasso to survive. He could just about afford his food and board and the basic materials he needed for his art. Several portraits of Manyac exist from this period. None of his work however, betrays the unique Picasso style which had yet to emerge.

After two months in Paris, Picasso returned to Barcelona with Casagemas. He had become even more alienated from his parents during his time abroad. They now had great difficulty accepting his Bohemian appearance and avant-garde opinions and were forced to abandon their idea of fame through their son who had failed them as a sound academic artist. Casagemas had become miserable too, a victim of unrequited love. The joint influences of a depressive friend and disapproving parents prompted Picasso to move on to Madrid after only a fortnight in Barcelona. Here he met up with a writer-friend, Francisco de Assis Soler, and the two produced a magazine together entitled *Arte Joven*. Picasso took charge of the artwork, while Soler acted as literary editor, and he filled the magazine's pages with drawings and satirical cartoons of Spanish life, prostitutes, street scenes and portraits of its two founders. Only two or three editions of the magazine were published, however. There was very little money available to keep it going and, at the same time, Picasso received disturbing news of his friend's tragic death. Carlos Casagemas had shot himself in a Parisian café because the woman he loved would not return his affection.

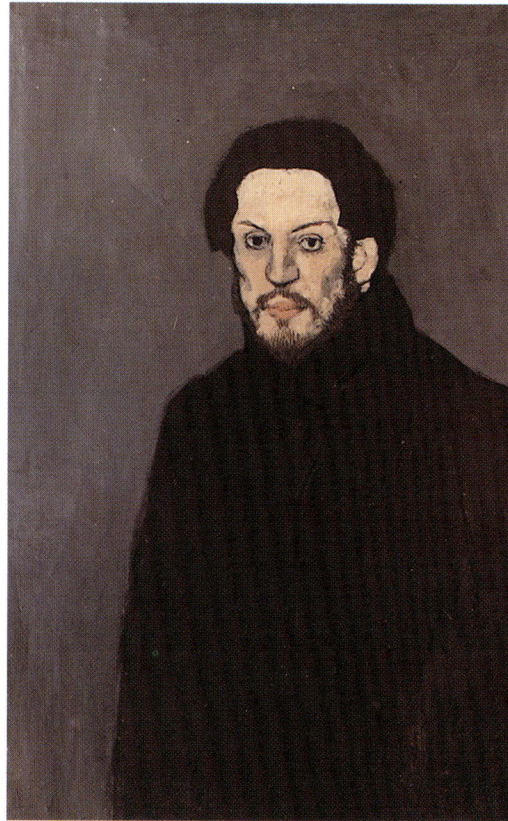

Self-Portrait, **1901 (Musée Picasso, Paris)** Picasso was about to enter his Blue Period when he painted this portrait. It reflects the poverty and despair he experienced in those first few years as a struggling young artist in Paris.

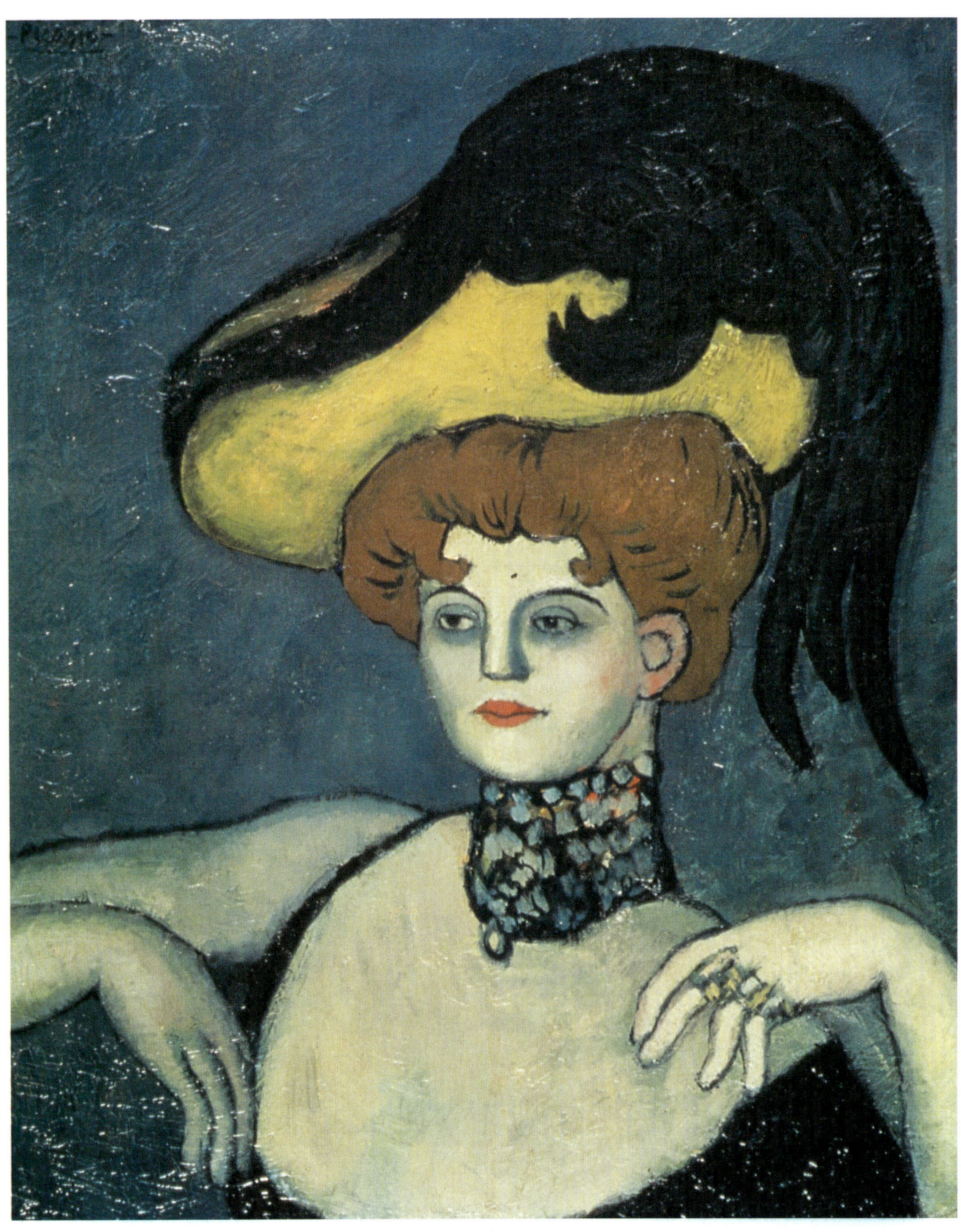

Picasso's patron in Paris, Pedro Manyac, had not forgotten his contract with the young artist. He wrote to him in Spain demanding the pictures he had been promised, but he was more anxious to persuade his young protégé to return to the city he had left behind. Picasso was increasingly unhappy with Spain's provincialism and did not hesitate, therefore, when Manyac offered him the opportunity to exhibit a collection of his works in Paris at a forthcoming event in June, 1901. Picasso left Madrid and returned to Barcelona to prepare for his Paris exhibition. He combined all the painting techniques he had learned in Paris with typically Spanish subjects, bull-fights, peasants, Spanish landscapes with churches, views of the Costa Brava. Before he left for Paris, he was invited to exhibit at the Salon Pares in Barcelona. His work was very well received at this event. Miguel Utrillo wrote a glowing account of his achievements in the *Pel y Ploma* journal and the article was accompanied by a portrait of Picasso, painted by Ramon Casas.

Manyac allowed Picasso to share his studio at the Boulevard de Clichy when he returned to Paris for the second time and also introduced him to the art dealer Ambroise Vollard. The latter was to become one of the most influential dealers in Paris, eventually satisfying the demands of some of the most prominent museums and galleries world-wide. Picasso energetically plunged himself into his work and awaited the exhibition which was to be held at Vollard's gallery at rue Laffitte. He painted such works as *The Flower Seller, The Diners, Bullfight, Harlequin,* and *Boulevard de Clichy* during this time. Vollard had acquired a reputation for presenting unconventional artists to the public. Cézanne's paintings had been on show at the same small gallery in 1895 and had been criticized for exceeding 'the boundaries of legally permissible practical jokes'. Picasso, at nineteen, was about to experience a similar flood of critical attention.

Seventy-five of the young artist's works were put on display. It had taken Picasso less than a year to acquaint himself with a diverse range of fashionable techniques, he had mastered the art of colour and perspective, projecting a level of experience far beyond his years. Fame was almost certain, nobody could deny that he was a genuine painter of outstanding talent, yet he could not accept his future as an artist on these terms. The reviews of his work were more than encouraging, but there was one which seemed to echo precisely what Picasso had increasingly begun to feel within himself. In *La Revue Blanche*, Felicien Fagus had pointed out that Picasso's 'passionate surge forward' had not 'left him the leisure to forge for himself a personal style'. He remained unchallenged and discouraged. Paris, once a source of learning and inspiration, now induced feelings of loneliness, isolation and a weariness which demanded expression. Casagemas was dead, grief refused to be contained. Images of poverty and austerity swiftly invaded the disillusioned world of an artist desperately struggling towards self-awareness.

Courtesan with Jewelled Collar, **1901 (Los Angeles County Museum)** Picasso paid more attention to outline and the use of vivid colour under the influence of Gauguin, whom he met in 1901. This painting was one of the last to use a mixture of colours, instead of simply blue.

CHAPTER 2

The Blue and the Rose (1901-1906)

Picasso's Blue Period arrived decisively and unapologetically. With a fierce determination that was to become his unique signature, Picasso turned his back on popular success and all that he had achieved, refusing to consider the material consequences of such a decision.

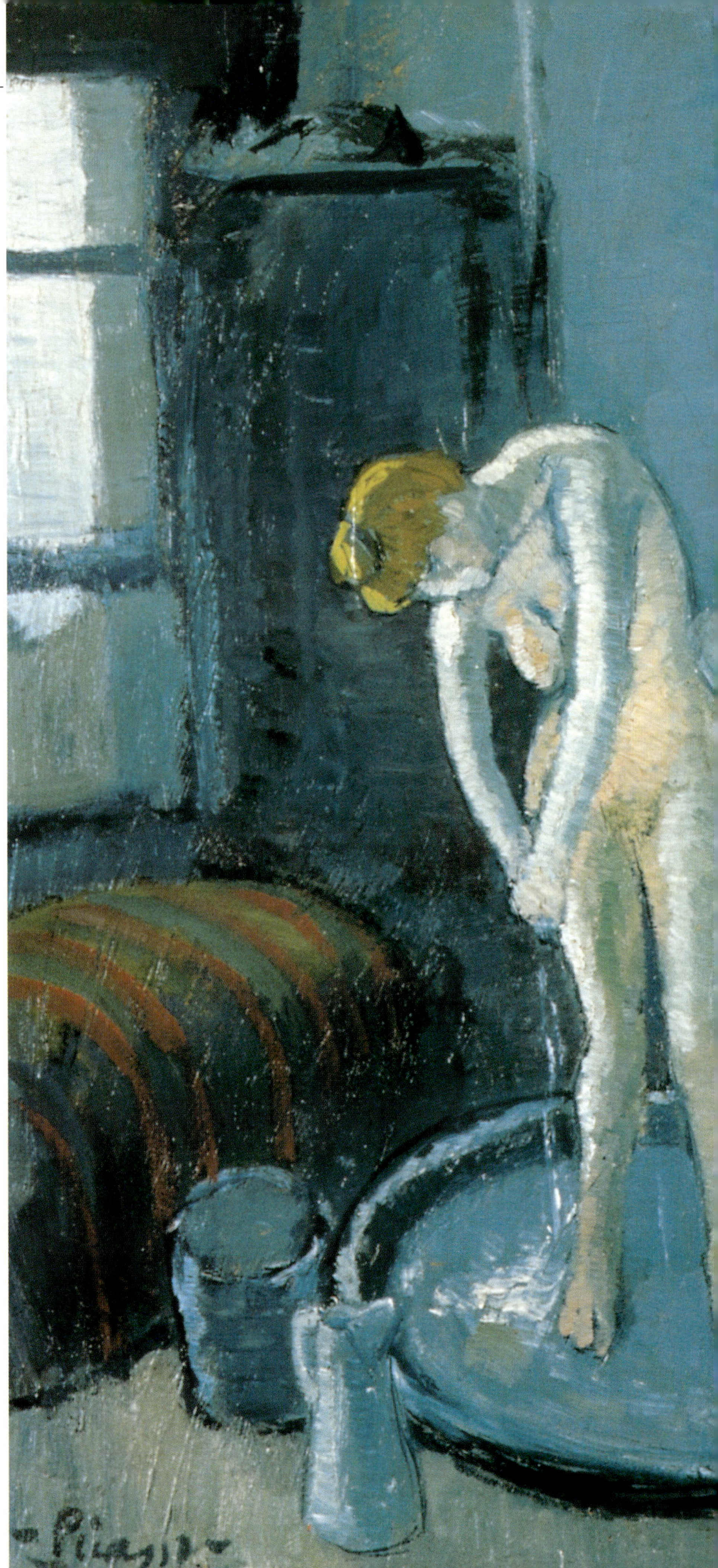

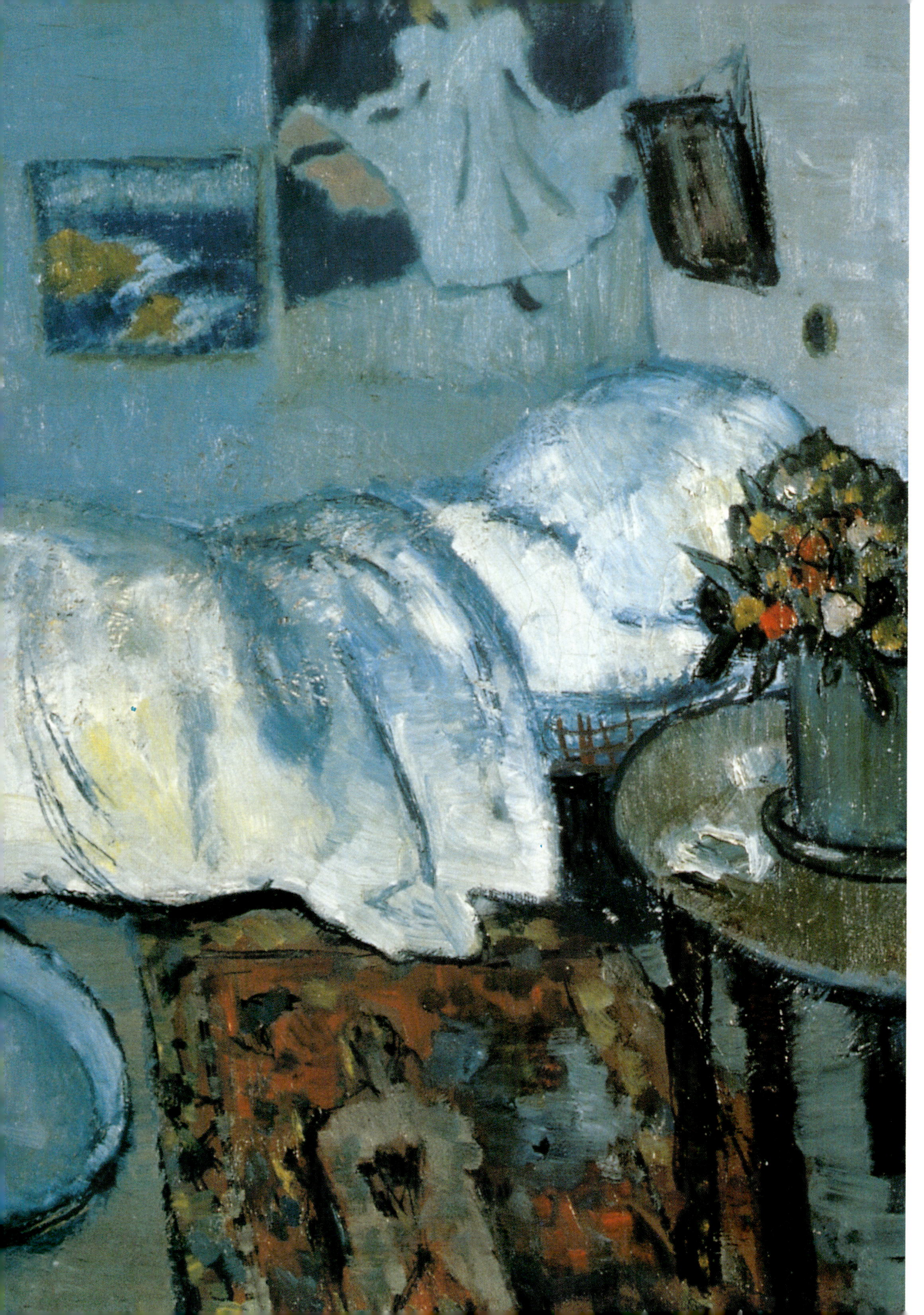

Overleaf:
The Blue Room, 1901 (Phillips Collection, Washington) All of the works of the Blue Period are moving and evocative, thematically linked by powerful feelings of gloom and despair. This painting, immortalizing his cramped attic accommodation, is not yet entirely monochrome, but Picasso eventually eradicated the cheerful associations of colour in the works to follow.

Opposite:
Poor People on the Seashore, 1903 (National Gallery, Washington) Picasso painted a whole series of works depicting ordinary people in circumstances of acute poverty. This painting, *Tragedy*, is one of the best known of the series.

By the end of the autumn 1901 Picasso had entered a world within himself, a desperately sorrowful and gloomy world, colouring his every outward perception and abruptly translating itself into art. A combination of circumstances seems to have induced the eruption of acute despair at this time. Picasso had arrived at an understanding of Parisian fame as mere entrapment and had rejected it on these grounds. In doing so, he invited a wretched poverty which dominated his early years in Paris. Now that his first major exhibition was over, the reality of Casagemas' suicide had also just begun to affect him deeply. The subjects of death and deprivation could no longer be ignored and the powerful combination of both experiences on a personal level helped sustain a blanket-depression, reflected in his paintings throughout the next four years – the artist's Blue Period.

Picasso stopped painting the gay streets of Paris, the colourful cafés, the cheerful rural and urban scenes of Spanish life, the representative portraits of his friends. He moved away from man's external world and now took man himself as his subject, including all his inner turmoil and difficulties. He moved from objectivity to subjectivity and blue seemed the most appropriate colour to express his feelings of sadness and anxiety. Van Gogh had been one of the first to choose his colours for their emotional impact and Picasso was now intent on following a similar route. As soon as he had arrived in Paris for the second time, Picasso had visited the retrospective exhibition of Van Gogh's work at Bernheim's, which undoubtedly gave him the confidence to allow his real self to emerge. At first, the blue was mixed with other sombre tones, but gradually the paintings of this period became increasingly monochrome in character.

'I began to paint in blue,' Picasso proclaimed in later life, 'when I realized that Casagemas had died.' His painting, *Evocation –The Burial of Casagemas,* which commemorated the death of his friend, heralded the beginning of the Blue Period. The picture is Picasso's attempt to come to terms with death through his art, a goal which he successfully achieved. He was undoubtedly influenced by Greco's painting *The Funeral of Count Orgaz,* and possibly used it as a model for his most ambitious work to date. The streaks of colour and the elongated bodies of this painting certainly mirror Greco's stylistic features. Although Picasso's subject is burial, and a sense of grief pervades, there is also an obvious element of humour and even redemption in this portrayal of death. Casagemas' suicide had been prompted by the discovery that he was impotent. He had declared his undying passion for his fiancée, yet had avoided every opportunity for physical intimacy, with the result that his lover had spurned him. The shrouded body is surrounded by a group of women mourning the departure of a loved one, but this tragic scene is counterpointed by the gathering of stocking-clad prostitutes, given an ethereal air as they float on a bed of clouds.

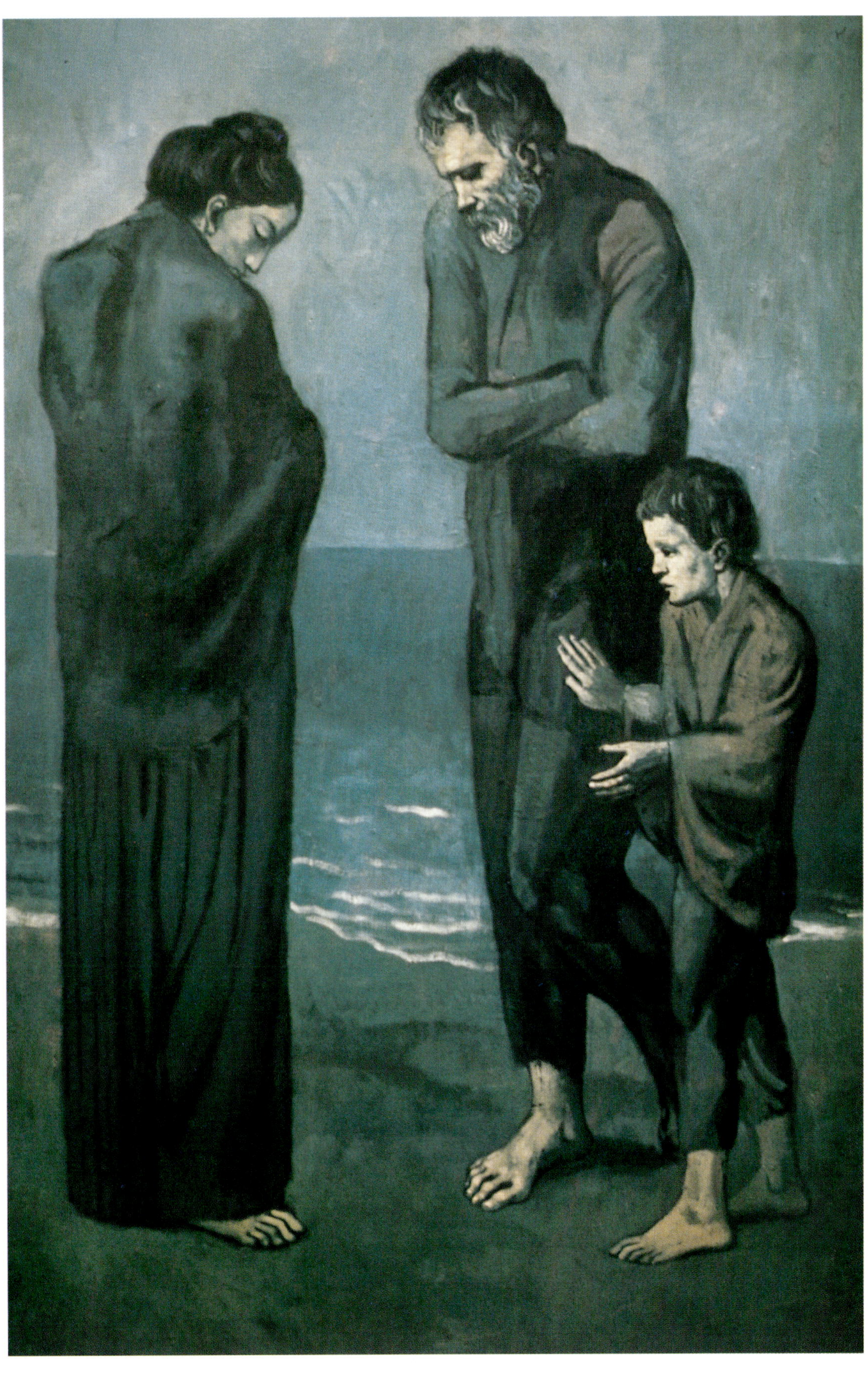

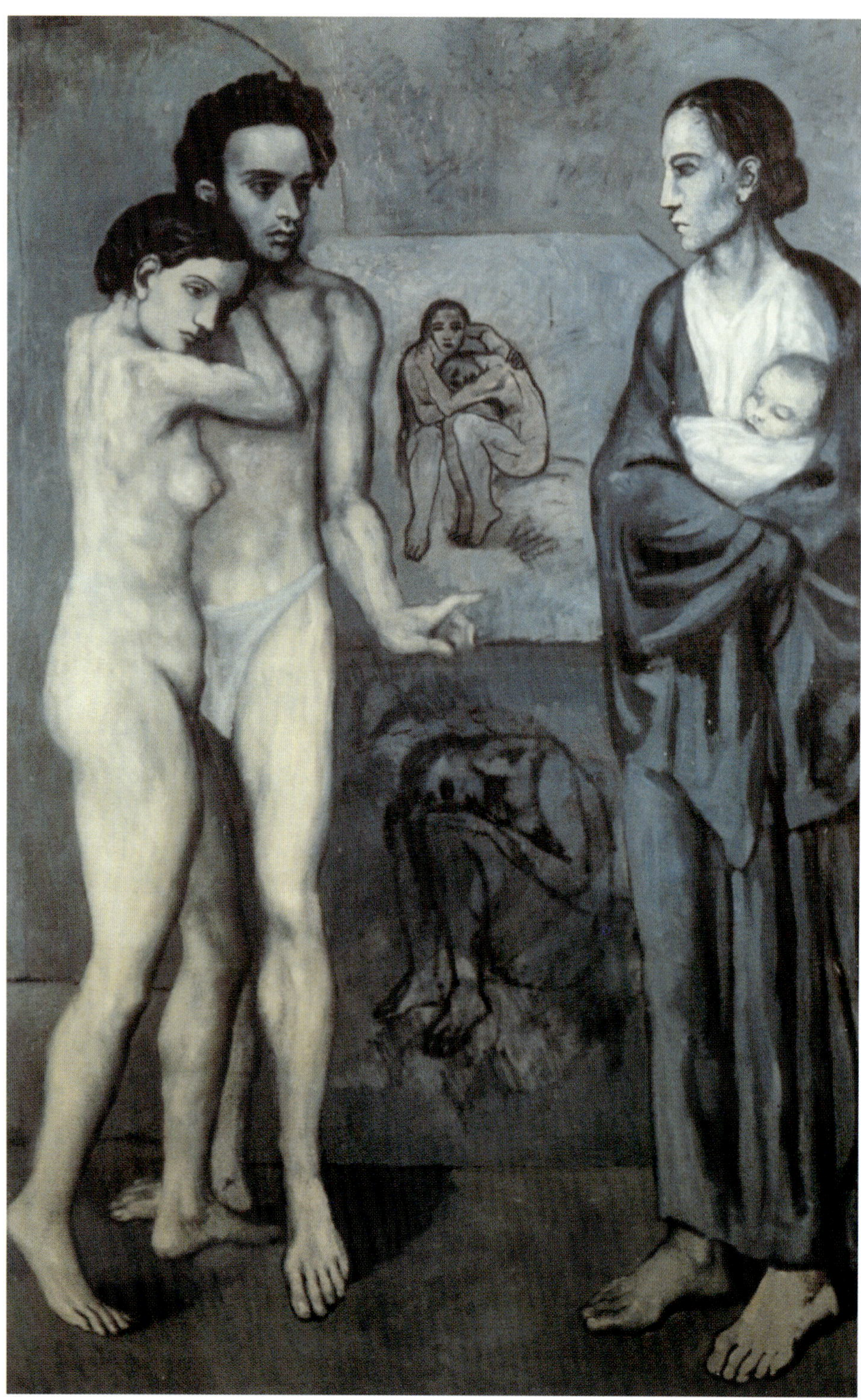

La Vie, **1903 (Cleveland Museum of Art)** One of Picasso's more enigmatic works of the Blue Period which seems to offer an allegorical message. It is a deeply moody painting, featuring a cycle-of-life theme, popular at the turn of the century.

They are Picasso's sardonic representation of an angelic presence, waiting to take charge of the spirit of the dead man and grant him those carnal pleasures denied him on earth.

A particularly miserable winter followed Picasso's painting of Casagemas. Themes of death, sorrow and isolation dominated his work. His melancholic mood was no doubt inspired by artists like Van

Gogh, whose life had ended in tragedy, but also by the premature death that summer of Henri de Toulouse-Lautrec – a man he much admired – at the age of thirty-seven. In December 1901 Picasso met the artist, Gauguin. They became good friends and saw each other almost daily. Picasso was influenced by Gauguin's desire to express his inner experience through his art by means of more simplified shapes, expressive colours and distinctively heavy black outlines. *Child with a Pigeon*, *Seated Nude* and *Courtesan with Jewelled Collar* are three examples of Picasso's development towards more expressive lines and decisive contours under the direct influence of Paul Gauguin and his own sense of personal tragedy. During these months, he also completed a portrait of his friend, Jaime Sabartés, a work often referred to as *The Bock*, and he painted *The Blue Room*. One of Picasso's first self-portraits, painted at this time in bold, forceful strokes, depicts a young man shrouded in blue, with a gaunt, pale face, gazing forward with an intense and purposeful expression. The painting reflects the poverty of the young Bohemian artist, but also the chill resolve to combat the penury of his circumstances. It is a stark and powerfully haunting portrait.

Picasso's new self-vision did not appeal to his patron, Manyac, or to Manyac's collectors. The relationship between the two men had become difficult as a result of Picasso's sudden change of style and Manyac now accepted very few of the artist's paintings. Picasso could not sell his work elsewhere, he could not even persuade any gallery to house them while he contemplated travelling back to Spain. His patron had discontinued his monthly payments and he was now facing virtual starvation. Under these circumstances, Barcelona had tremendous appeal and Picasso left Paris at the end of December, 1901, abandoning many of his early works of the Blue Period, in order to return to the comforts of a family home and three square meals a day. The departure from Paris also offered him the chance to regain some of his artistic liberty and a sense of his own identity, free of the disapproval of a fickle Parisian public.

Picasso remained in Barcelona from January to October 1902 and then returned to Paris for a short stay of six months, accompanied by his friend, Sebastian Junyer-Vidal. While on this third trip to Paris, until the spring of 1903, he changed his accommodation three times. He shared his final residence with the poet Max Jacob. Life was particularly miserable for both of them. Picasso would work all night while Max Jacob slept in the single bed. During the daytime, the roles were reversed and it was Picasso's turn to get some sleep. The tiny studio room was reputed to be so cold that Picasso burnt many of his paintings and watercolours in order to keep a fire going. Little of his work remains from this period, although it is certain that he again painted in blue, producing paintings which dwelt on the stigma of poverty. He was probably too destitute to afford a variety of colours, in any case.

Woman and Child on a Beach, 1902
(Christie's, London) The mother and
child theme was a favourite with
Picasso. He returned to it, more
cheerfully, during his Cubist phase and
it also manifested itself in his
Neoclassical paintings much later on.

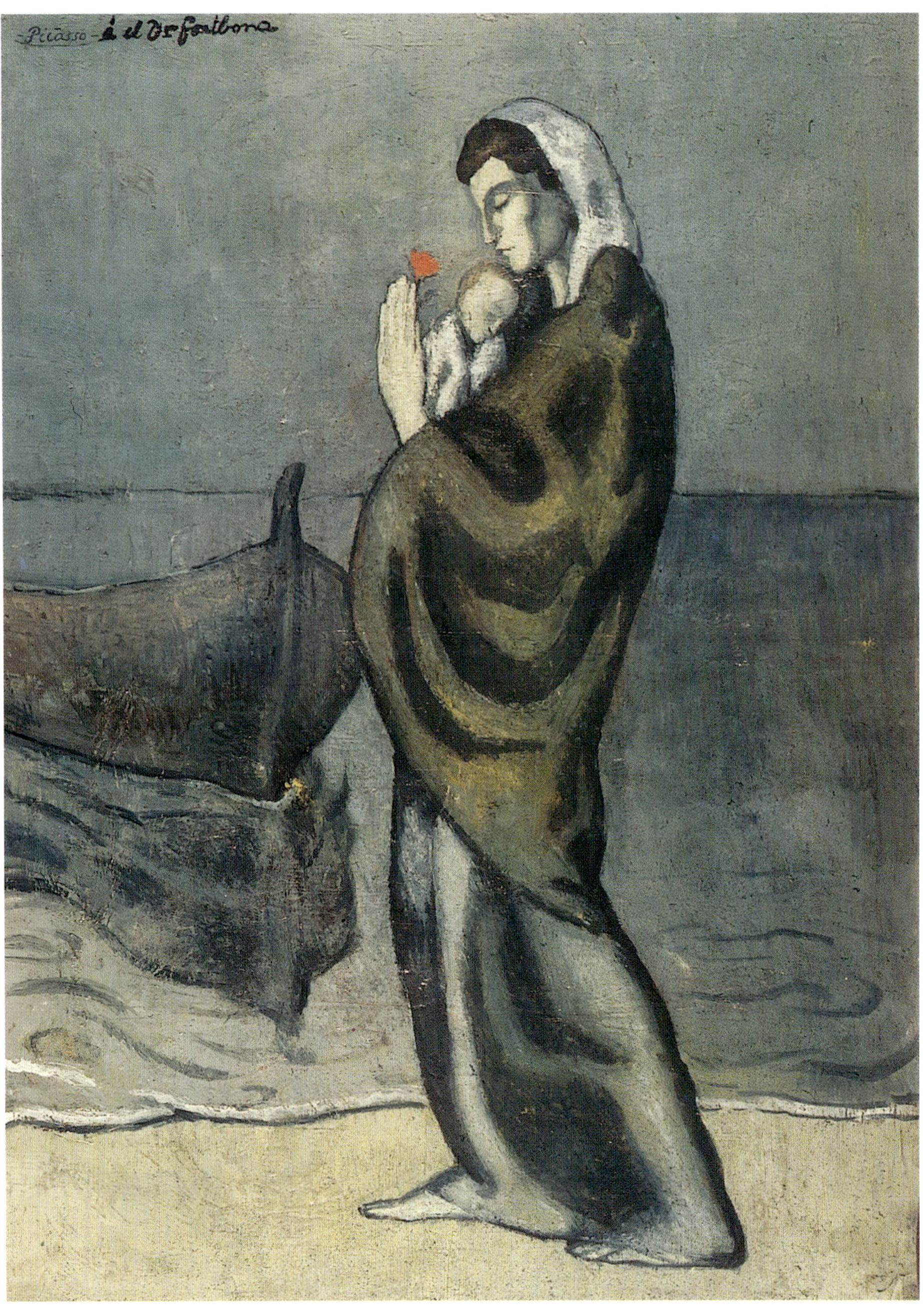

Opposite:
Portrait of Sebastian Junyer-Vidal,
1903 (Los Angeles County Museum)
Junyer-Vidal accompanied Picasso on
two of his early trips to Paris. This
painting foreshadows *The Frugal Repast*
in its subject matter and café setting, but
does not radiate the same terrifyingly
haunting despondency of the later
piece.

The loneliness and hardship of *The Absinthe Drinker* or *Squatting Woman*, painted at this time, call to mind familiar themes first explored in the works of Van Gogh.

Picasso eventually returned to Spain where he remained for over a year. He resumed painting in the same melancholic mood. He had ceased to reach towards new influences, but continued to favour an emotional expression of the misery he witnessed around him and had experienced himself at first hand. He combined realism with a shift towards mannerism, a technique employing characteristic distortion and exaggeration of human proportions, achieving a unique style of his own. He had learned to draw the human figure with astounding

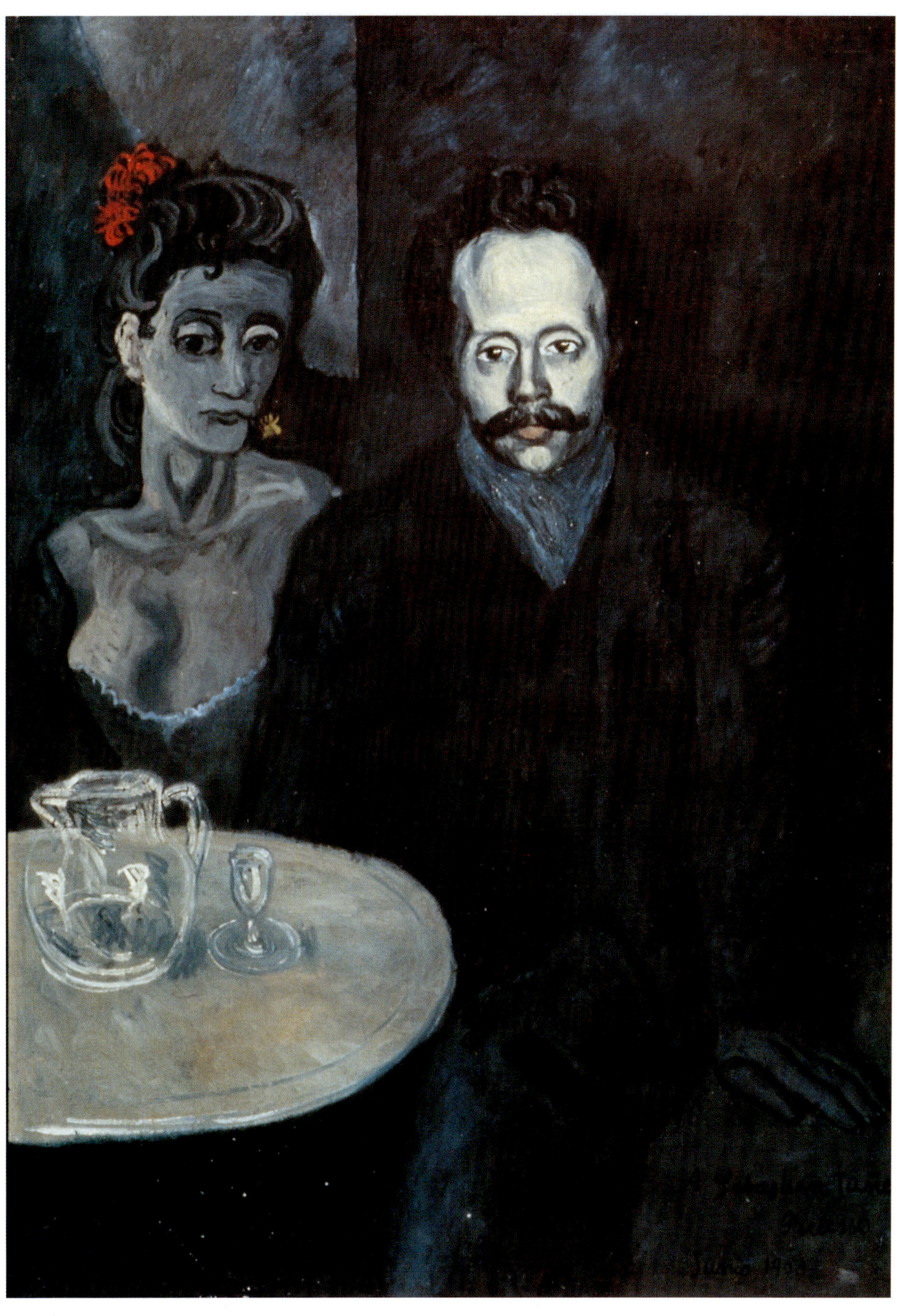

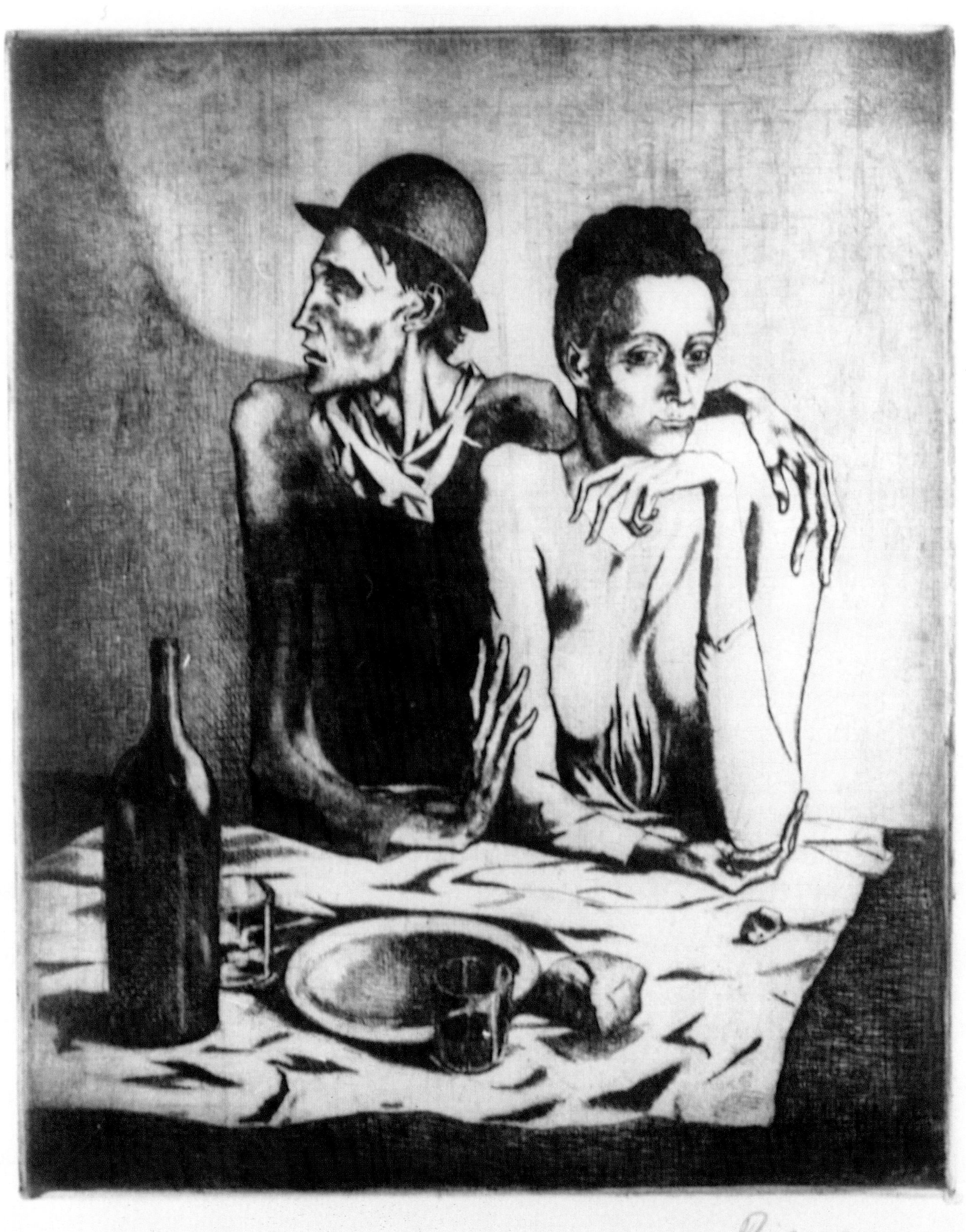

precision as a young adolescent, now it became distorted as a means to portray the moral and physical hemiplegia of his subjects. He could scarcely avoid the issue of poverty in the works which were to follow. Its co-existence alongside the wealth he encountered in well-to-do areas of Paris, and also Barcelona, led to many paintings of either prostitutes in an abyss of degradation, or ordinary people in the grip of despondency, driven to begging and utter exhaustion. At this time, he was living at home and surviving on a pittance from his parents. His own poverty seems to have affected him only superficially and his year in Spain proved to be one of the most fruitful periods of his life to date. He hired a small studio with two friends and thrived in the atmosphere of creative chaos. He found disorder stimulating and began to paint an entire series of masterpieces. Over a period of fourteen months he painted over fifty pictures. The poet Guillaume Apollinaire, with whom Picasso had a long-standing friendship, described Picasso's work of the Blue Period as 'damp painting, blue like the wet bottom of the abyss, and pitiful'. A silent, strange world emerged from his paintbrush, each canvas emanating a profound human sympathy. His paintings were populated by skeletal, sexless, hungry-looking individuals, bony, squalid beggars, frail old men and women, whole families, miserable and detached, or wretched couples without intimacy, all portrayed with tapering fingers or elongated limbs, against an increasingly simplified, bleak, blue background.

During 1903, Picasso completed many of the most well known works of his Blue Period. There is no trace of still-life in the paintings produced in Barcelona, Picasso was preoccupied only with man, buried in a climate of suffering. Some of the outstanding works produced include *The Old Jew, The Old Guitar Player, The Embrace, La Soupe,* the sequence *Les Pauvres au bord de la mer* (Poor People on the Seashore), *Soler Family's Picnic* and *La Vie. Tragedy – Les Pauvres au bord de la mer* depicts a family frozen in time, utterly lacking in warmth both physically – as indicated by the barefoot man clutching his overcoat closer to him for protection from the weather, and equally towards each other – where each figure stands separately without making any form of physical contact, or even eye contact. Only the small child makes a pitiful, pleading gesture, somehow managing to hold his head up. The use of monochrome renders these figures timeless and independent of location. Poverty is unconcealed, as is the cruel absence of love within the family relationship.

La Vie is a more enigmatic and studied piece. It was not a spontaneous painting and Picasso put a good deal of thought into its creation, planning it as early as the spring of 1903 and making several preliminary sketches before applying paint to canvas. *La Vie* consists of four distinct units which together form an entire cycle-of-life scene, although the overall impression is one of uncomfortable disjointedness.

The Frugal Repast (**Musée Picasso, Paris**) Picasso created this engraving in 1904 and many judge it to be the dramatic climax of his Blue Period. He never again produced scenes of poverty which made such a savage impact on the viewer.

The setting is the artist's studio. Early sketches contained the painter's easel, but this has been removed from the finished painting. The sketches also reveal that Picasso was originally the central figure of the painting. The androgynous-looking mother figure to the right of the canvas was initially a stooped old man, representing the artist as an older man. The young man portrayed is not Picasso, although X-rays of the work reveal that this was at first a self-portrait. The final figure of the young man is another portrait of Casagemas and the naked female bears a striking resemblance to Germaine, the woman who could not return Casagemas' love.

The theme of the painting appears to be love, or rather, the unhappiness love can bring. Sexual love, motherly love, platonic love, and a life without love are all represented in the painting. The naked, standing couple who embody carnal love radiate a sense of its hollowness. There is an atmosphere of remoteness between them, the young woman has flung her arms woefully around her lover. The mother figure stands apart and stares reproachfully at the young couple. The harshness of life is reflected in her face and she seems to announce the existence of misery from birth, symbolized by the baby she holds in her arms, right through to death. The foetal position of the man or woman in the lower background canvas separating the standing figures, re-enforces a theme of isolation and despair from the very outset of life. The sexless figure radiates exhaustion, perhaps a loss of love. The figures in the smaller painting above it, demand reassurance. If the female in this figure is Germaine, as some believe, she seems frightened, even repentant, and also cowers beneath the penetrating stare of the cloaked woman, depicted with huge, masculine feet.

La Vie was sold only a few days after completion, and Picasso, after many years of poverty, seems to have been struck by the idea of earning a proper living from his paintings. This situation however, was still quite a long way off. *La Vie* was neither exhibited nor published at this time, but his friend and fellow painter, Sebastian Junyer-Vidal, triumphantly announced the sale in an article published in *El Liberal*, helping to improve Picasso's standing and fame in the Barcelona art world after quite a long absence from the public eye. The article stated:

> *The painting ... entitled* La Vie, *is one of those works which can at a stroke establish an artist's name and reputation. The subject is interesting and provocative, and the conception is of such strength and intensity that it is without a doubt one of the few truly impressive works to have been created in Spain for some time.*

In April 1904, Picasso made the decision to return to Paris. This was his fourth trip and he was to settle there permanently on this occasion. He journeyed from Barcelona once again with Junyer-Vidal. A

The Travelling Artists, **1905 (Musée Picasso, Paris)** The Rose Period paintings reintroduced a liveliness of tone and subject matter to Picasso's paintings. He began to paint scenes from circus life, which although melancholic at times, did not dwell exclusively on a theme of human suffering.

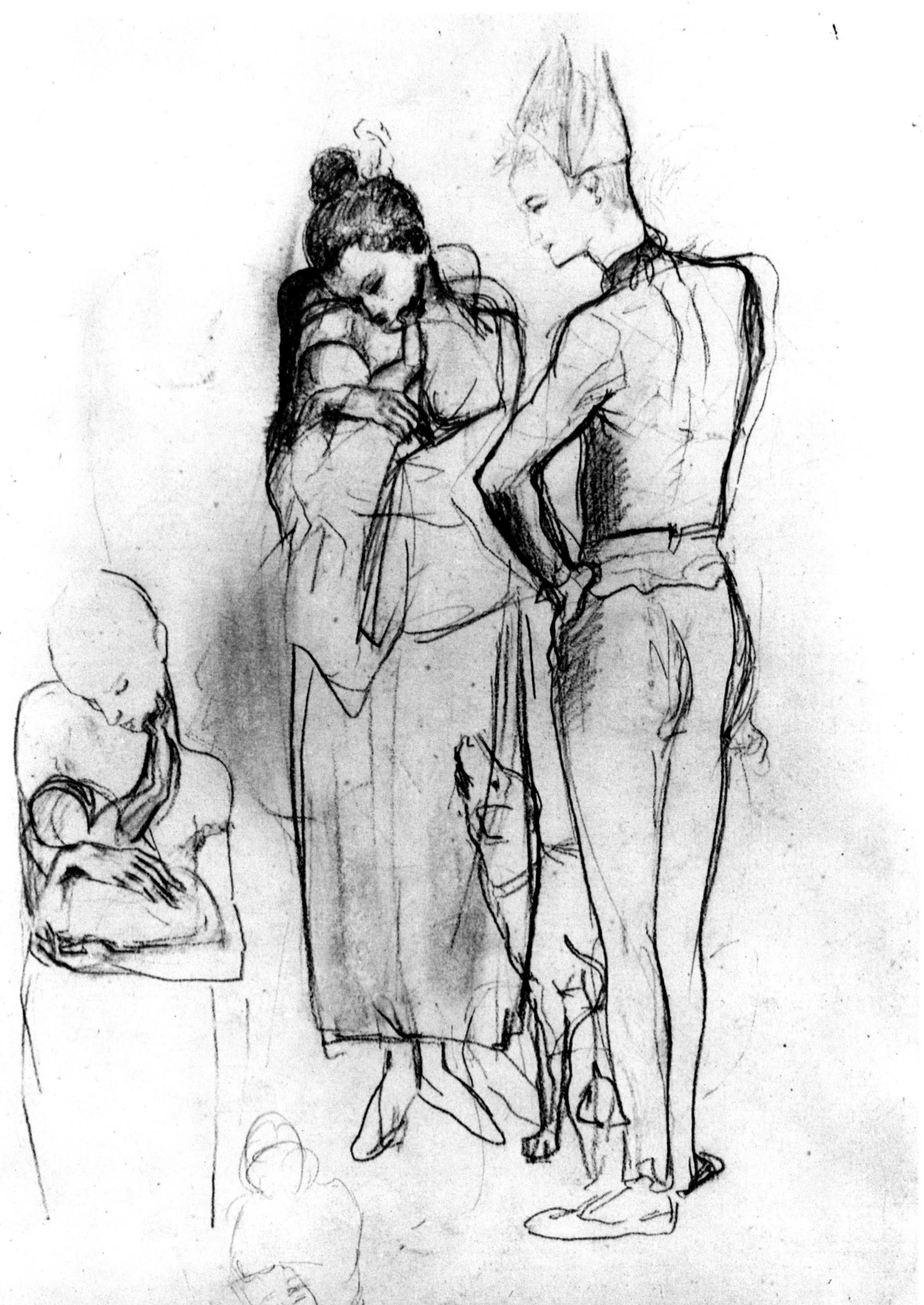

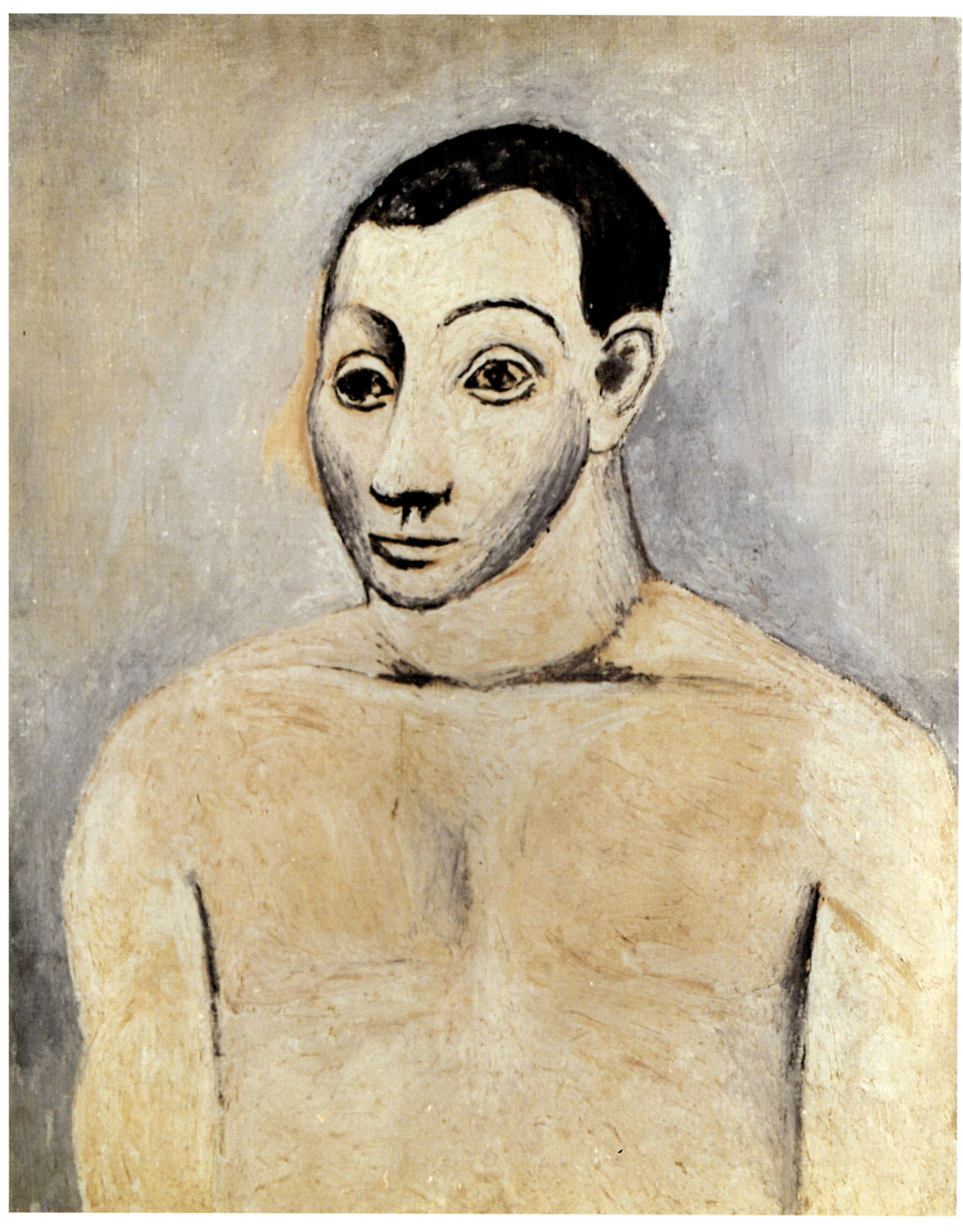

sculptor friend, Paco Durio, allowed him to use his studio in the 'Bateau Lavoir', christened after the laundry barges anchored in the river Seine, and he remained here until October 1909. Picasso was still as poor as the people of his Blue paintings, the studio contained very little furniture and very few domestic comforts. Displays of high living and lavish spending in the wealthy quarters of Paris contrasted sharply with the lifestyles of artists in the Montmartre region of the city, where even necessities were beyond the painter's purse. Picasso's last great masterpiece of this Blue Period was *The Frugal Repast*, his first true engraving, which took him several months to complete. He was first introduced to the art of print-making as early as 1899, at the age of eighteen when he met Ricard Canals in his native Spain. It was a field Picasso would transform more radically than any other artist in the fullness of time. He rapidly assimilated the techniques of this art form and produced an etching entitled *El Zurdo* (The Left-handed Man). The subject of the print was a picador with an owl at his feet, holding a pike in his right hand. Picasso christened it *El Zurdo* because his picador emerged holding his pike in his left hand. He had failed to consider that the image would be reversed in the final print.

The Frugal Repast was drawn with almost savage strokes of the etching needle and exudes a terrifyingly brutal reality. Picasso could not afford the copper usually employed in the medium of engraving and had to make do with an old zinc block, still showing traces of a landscape worked on by another artist. His subjects are a man and a woman sitting at a table in a dreary café. An intense feeling of sordid poverty and alcoholism pervades the grey atmosphere. Both figures appear wretched and starving. The man's gaze is averted, his bony fingers attempt to embrace the woman who stares despondently into space. Picasso was very fond of this work, it was one of the first pieces he showed to Fernande Olivier, a woman who would dramatically alter his life and his art. He had prints taken and distributed them to his friends. He produced 257 engravings between 1899 and 1931 alone, and went on to produce many more. Picasso's engravings equal the virtuosity of his paintings. The series of etchings he completed in 1905, entitled *The Acrobats*, are some of the most prized of his works and the plates are much sought after.

In spite of his impoverished circumstances in the 'Bateau-Lavoir', Picasso made many new friends, including the poet and critic, Guillaume Apollinaire. The circle of artistic friends would meet in *Le Lapin Agile*, united by a sense of their alienation from an indifferent and selfish Parisian society, and by a belief in their own creative gifts which sustained them through extremely difficult times. Ambroise Vollard bought a canvas from time to time, but Picasso had no form of regular income. Fortunately for the young artists, the landlord of *Le Lapin Agile* accepted paintings as payment for food and drink and at this time

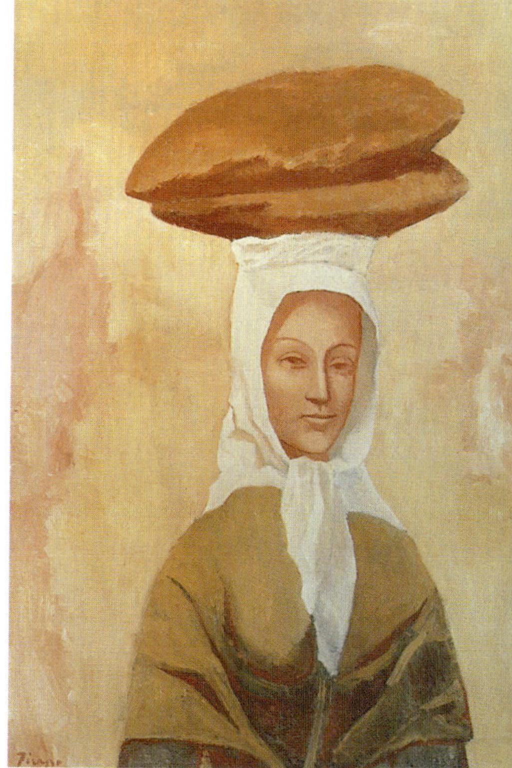

***Woman with a Loaf of Bread* (Philadelphia Museum).** Many attribute Picasso's break from the Blue Period to Fernande Olivier, who seemed to dispel his sombre mood. This painting demonstrates the perfect balance achieved between the human and the traditional approach to the portrayal of peasant life.

Opposite:
***Self-Portrait*, 1906 (Musée Picasso, Paris)** There is a remarkable difference between this and the self-portrait painted in 1901, when Picasso was entering his Blue Period. The self-pitying, introspective stare of the young artist in the grip of depression has all but disappeared. Simplified facial features, characteristic of primitive art, are now very apparent. The influences of Iberian sculpture are particularly evident.

Picasso painted *Woman with a Crow*, a portrait of the landlord's daughter, executed in a now familiar style of elongation and distortion of the human form. Subtle changes appeared in this work, however. Only the background remains blue, while the slender young woman is gracefully painted in soft shades of amber, almost fading to pink. Apollinaire immediately published a glowing account of Picasso's work in *La Plume* magazine. The sense of acute misery disappeared from his paintings, his sombre mood lifted, and he entered the Rose Period which lasted until 1906.

Women had evidently begun to awaken his sensuality and in August 1904 he began an affair with Fernande Olivier, a woman with cascading red hair and green eyes, whom he had met in the Bateau Lavoir. They formed a relationship that survived for the next seven years. Picasso later described these years as some of the happiest of his life. They certainly proved decisive to his art. Under Fernande's influence, he began to show some slackening of tension. It was a full year however, before Fernande actually moved in with Picasso to share his tiny studio. On her first visit she was astonished by the sadness and disorder of Picasso's life and recorded these impressions in her memoirs, *Picasso and his Friends*:

> *Huge, unfinished canvases stood all over the studio and everything there suggested work: but, my God, what chaos! A cane chair, easels, canvases of every size and tubes of paint were scattered all over the floor with brushes, oil cans and a bowl for etching fluid. There were no curtains ... In winter the studio was so cold that the dregs of tea left in cups from the day before were frozen by morning. But the cold did not prevent Picasso from working without respite.*

Picasso turned away from blue and began to introduce more invigorating shades, including ochre, orange, red and pink. The subject matter of his work also changed. He no longer painted blind beggars, prostitutes and poverty-stricken families, but turned his attention towards the circus world. For a period of six months, harlequins, acrobats, tight-rope walkers and strolling performers became the focus of his attention, their portraits directly inspired by his visits to the bright pink tent of the Circus Medrano, situated a short distance from his lodgings in Montmartre. A touch of melancholy remains in these paintings, but the skeletal forms of the Blue Period are replaced by charmingly waif-like figures, radiating a humanity that is not overwhelmingly tragic.

The Family of Saltimbanques, a very large canvas, seven feet wide and seven feet high, which Picasso painted in 1905, remains one of his most impressive paintings of the Rose Period and one of the last to explore circus themes. The isolation of the artist was something to

Woman Combing her Hair (**Kimbell Art Museum, Fort Worth**) Picasso was beginning to apply the stylizations of primitive art to the full figure. He painted many nudes at this time, the majority of them bulky and basic in shape. Only the tinges of pink colour in these paintings connect them to the work of his Rose Period.

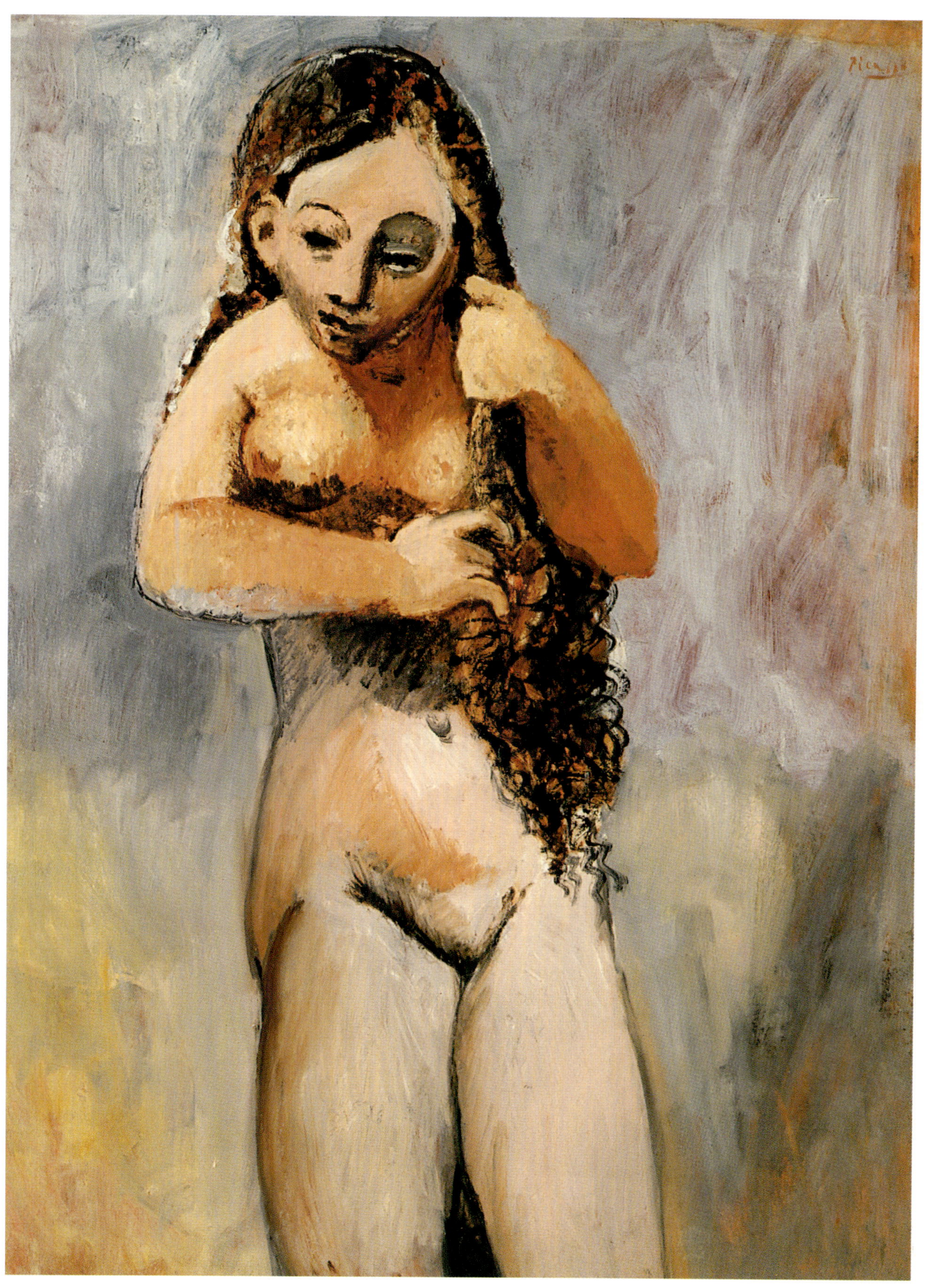

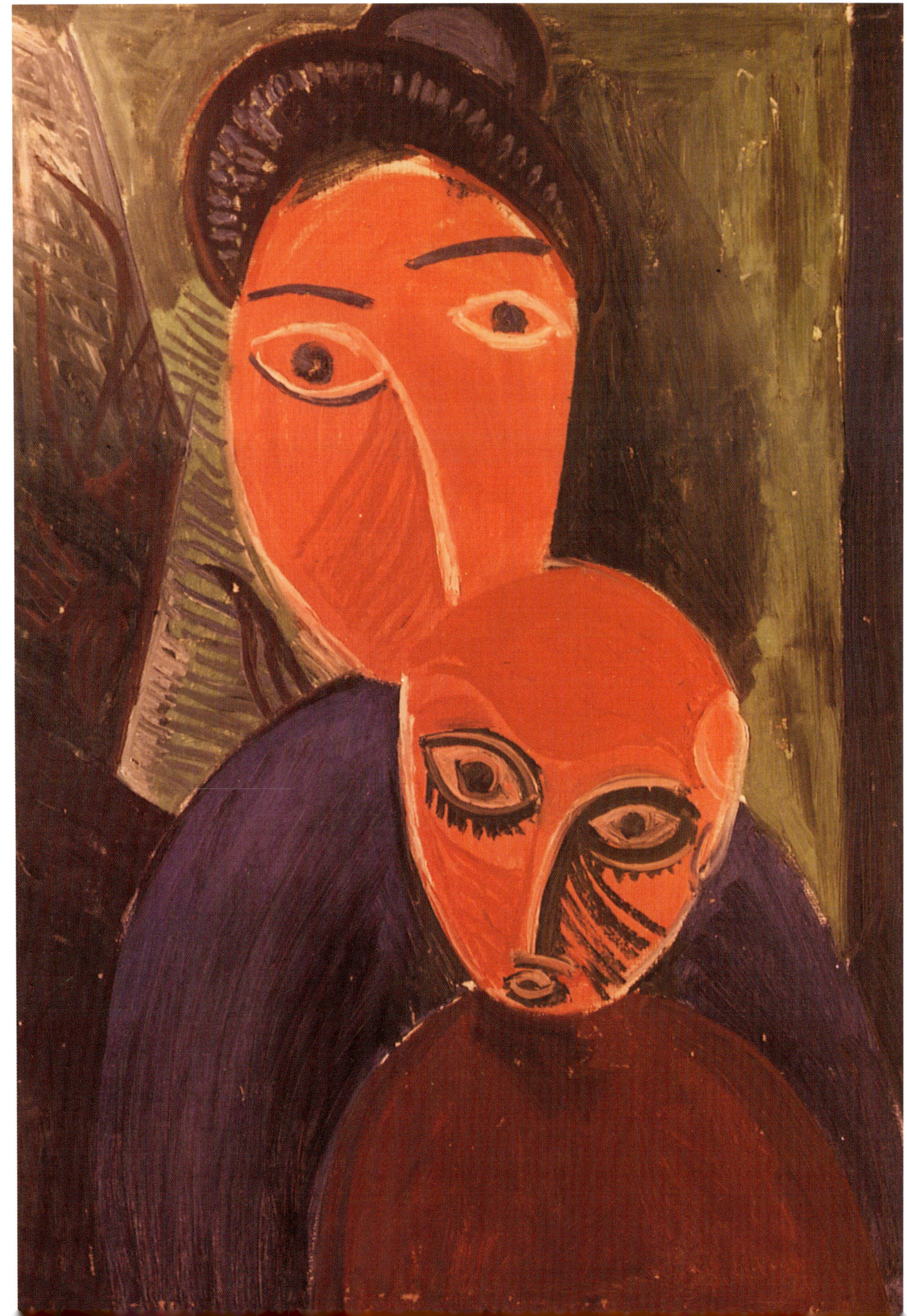

which Picasso could easily relate. The impression of poverty in this painting, when compared to the Blue Period, is rather more subtle and the elongated figures have all but disappeared, to be replaced by a more classical appreciation of form. Yet the itinerant acrobats exude a strained, enigmatic and solitary presence, suspended in time and place, set against a background that is both barren and desolate. The harlequin holds the little girl's hand, but their relationship does not appear easy. Her eyes are downcast and there is a distinct impression of separateness among all the figures in the painting.

After a trip to Holland in the summer of 1905, Picasso's Rose Period entered a new phase. His paintings after this visit contained less and less emotion, as he became preoccupied with purely plastic, or three-dimensional considerations. Picasso now judged his paintings too sentimental. He ruthlessly eliminated all elements of unreserved pathos from his work, focusing his attention almost exclusively on the figure itself, resolving to embrace a more objective view of his surroundings. He was heavily influenced by Apollinaire at this time, a young poet bent on total freedom of expression in his work, fired by an ambition to clear away old ideas for new ones in all the arts. Apollinaire's own verse reflected this practice in its unorthodox typography and utter disregard for conventional punctuation. Picasso's *Boy Leading a Horse*, painted in 1906, depicts a character whose face lacks emotion, the emphasis is on the figure alone. The personality remains buried and no specifics are offered, such as the earlier circus costumes, which might give the boy an identity of his own. *Woman with a Fan* displays a similar stiffening in approach and a simplification of form, resulting in a painting completely empty of sentiment. *La Toilette*, also painted in the same year, demonstrates the comfortable ease with which Picasso proved his expertise, making use of antique sources to produce a radical effect in his art.

By 1906, at the age of twenty-four, Picasso had achieved a status envied by most of his contemporaries. His paintings of the Blue Period had suddenly begun to attract attention and many were being sold to a rapidly expanding group of admirers. Two important collectors entered his life at this juncture, the wealthy German, Wilhelm Uhde, and the strong-willed American writer, Gertrude Stein. Gertrude had bought Picasso's *Girl with the Basket of Flowers*, knowing very little about the artist, but she was keen to discover more. She visited Picasso at his home with her brother Leo and purchased many more of his works, furnishing him with a sum of 800 francs, more than he had ever before held in his hand at any one time. Picasso offered to paint Gertrude's portrait, attracted by her mannish shoulders, her forceful personality and, no doubt, filled with a sense of gratitude. He invited her to his studio, little knowing that after over ninety sittings the portrait would still remain incomplete. Ambroise Vollard re-appeared at

Mother and Child, **1907 (Musée Picasso, Paris)** A comparison between this picture, and the painting, *Woman and Child on a Beach,* from the Blue Period, elucidates very clearly just how rapidly and dramatically Picasso had moved away from an emotional and realistic depiction of his surroundings, towards a Cubist style which would eventually ignore this.

this time also and bought thirty of Picasso's canvases, offering him 2000 francs. With this money, he decided to spend a holiday with Fernande in the Malagan village of Gosol. He had been away from his native country now for two years. A visit seemed appropriate and the two departed for Spain in the summer of 1906.

Friends and fellow artists undoubtedly expected Picasso to continue with his gentle Rose paintings which had finally brought him commercial success, yet, characteristically, he was already tiring of this phase. He had established himself as an extraordinarily talented painter and had produced over two hundred paintings, watercolours and pastels, together with hundreds of drawings in ink, crayon, charcoal and pencil. He had dabbled successfully in the media of sculpture, engraving and graphic art but, for all this, he remained unfulfilled, actively searching out new directions for his art. While in Gosol, he visited an exhibition of pre-Roman Iberian sculpture. He was immensely impressed by the simplification of form, accentuated features and powerful strength of these pieces. He began to adapt certain features of this art for his own purposes. Severe, symmetrical faces appeared in his paintings, many with large staring eyes. He began to use a terracotta colour to give his work greater depth and an earthy atmosphere. He also produced several sculptures and woodcuts while in Gosol in a spirit of primitivism, including the woodcut, *Head of Fernande*. He returned to Paris and explored his newly discovered passion further, visiting a number of exhibitions of primitive African art. He finished the portrait of Gertrude Stein without using her as model. The sculptural look of Stein's portrait – the stony set of her features and hardness of the hair – can only be attributed to Picasso's encounter with Iberian art. The self-portrait painted upon his return also reflects the same influence. It is in total contrast to the one painted during his Blue Period in 1901. In the 1906 portrait, completed when he was twenty-five, the artist's face and figure are simplified into crude, bulky shapes, reflecting the new vocabulary of primitive art.

Picasso's circle of friends now included Henri Matisse and André Derain, two leading supporters of Fauvism, with its belief that colour must have an absolutely supreme place in art. He also associated with Juan Gris and Georges Braque, both of whom would play a crucial role in his future. This group was intent on shaking the traditional foundations of art as a whole. Picasso began to apply some of the stylizations, evident in his later self-portrait, to the full figure. Among the many terracotta coloured paintings he now produced, *Two Nudes* and *Nude Boy* emphasize a very basic form of the human body. Picasso next began work on a series of sketches, with a view to producing an unorthodox composition, unlike any the art world had ever seen before. *Les Desmoiselles d'Avignon*, a painting of five women in a brothel, would irrevocably alter the face of modern art.

Nude with a Towel, 1907 (**Private Collection**) Picasso's female in this painting is portrayed in a manner very close to his nudes in *Les Desmoiselles d'Avignon*. Wedge-shaped features have been introduced. Breasts, facial characteristics and body contours are delineated by single, thick strokes of the paintbrush.

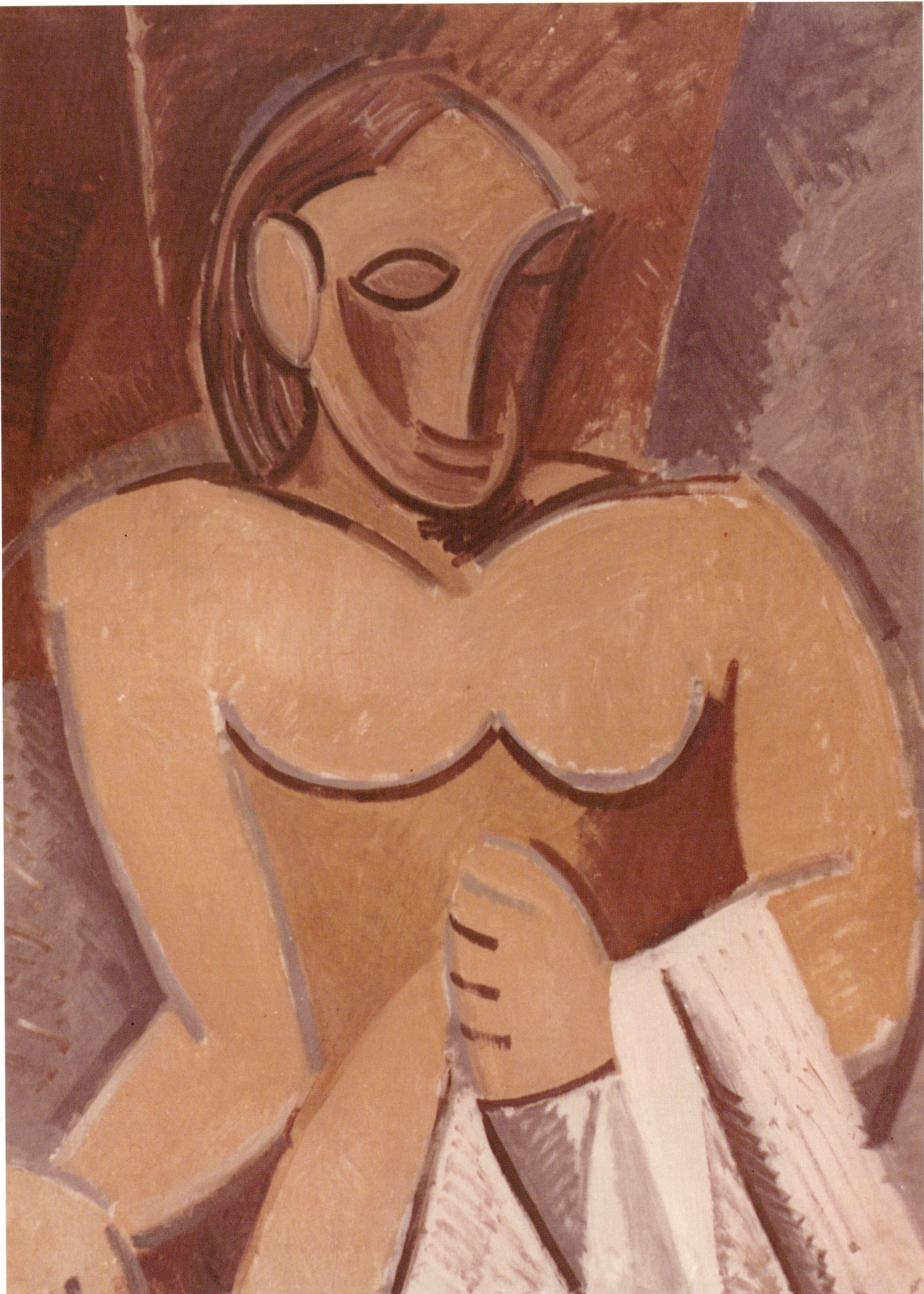

CHAPTER 3

Cubism and Beyond

If pressed to identify Picasso's single most important artistic achievement, one would have to say that it was his invention of a style eventually known as Cubism.

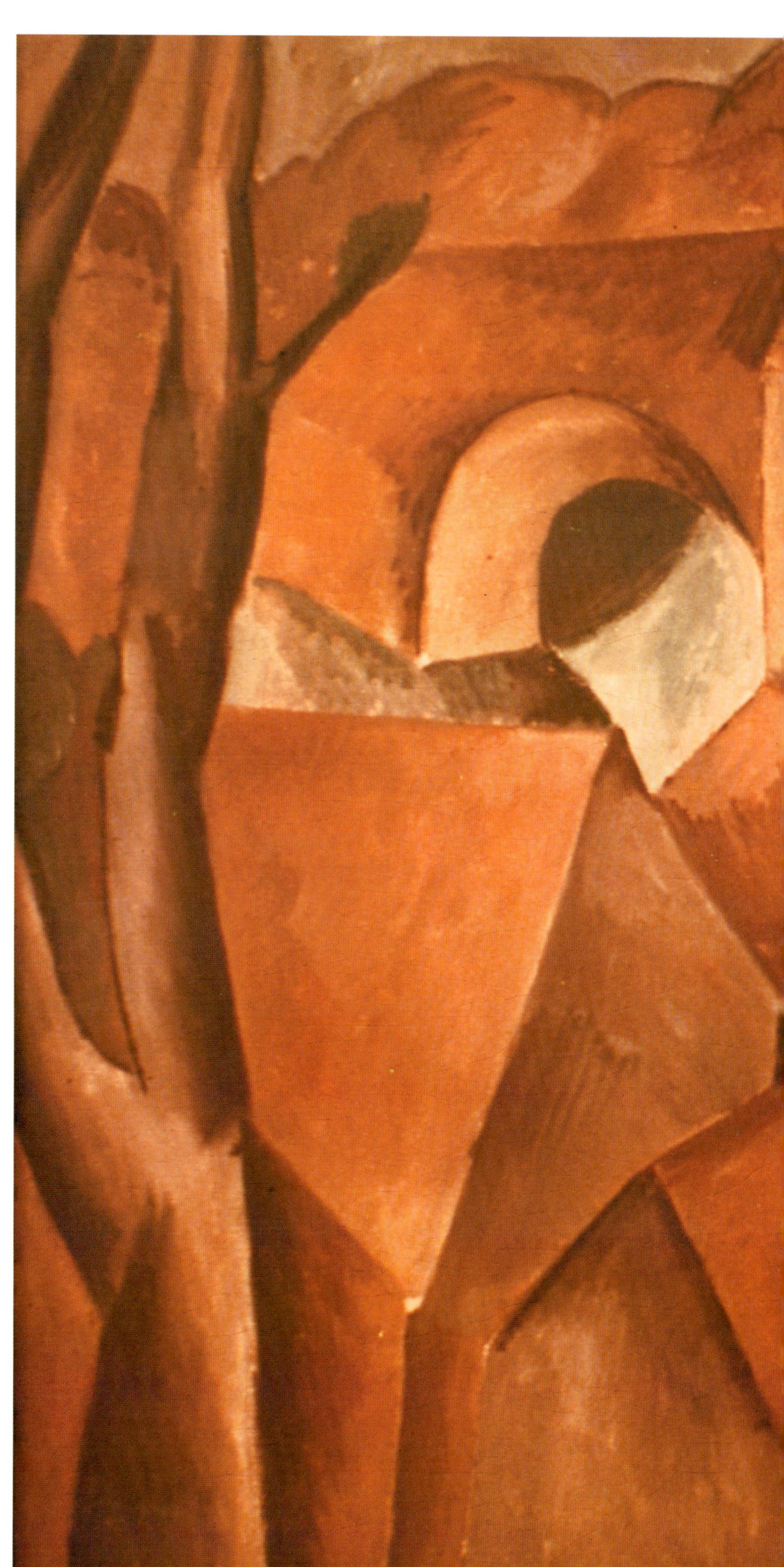

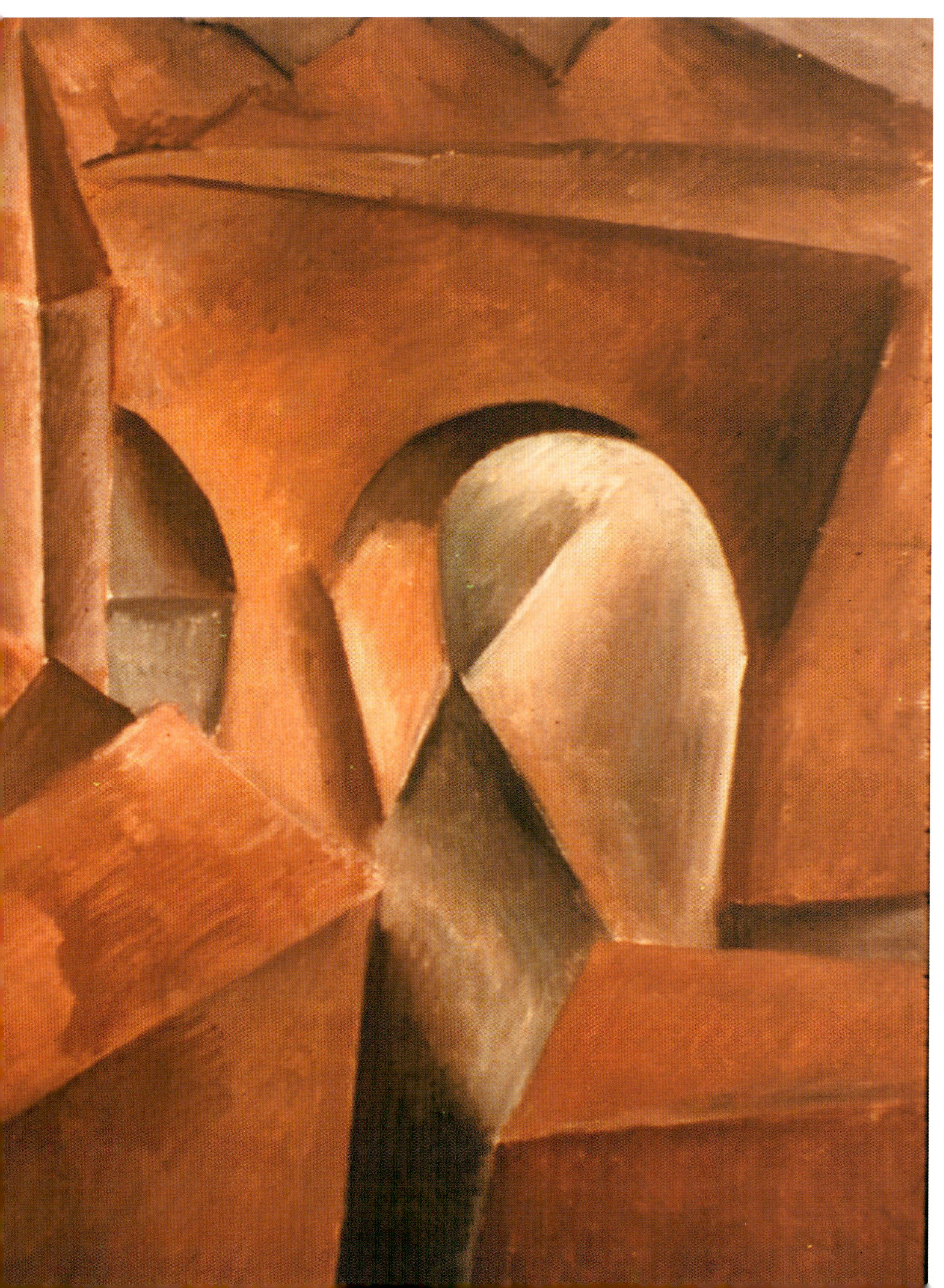

Overleaf:
Landscape with Bridge, 1909 (National Gallery, Prague) Picasso's landscapes of this period were usually painted in flat tones, such as ochre, and the austere Spanish landscape, in particular, lent itself to the Cubist style of eliminating detail, in favour of pure geometric solids and planes.

Opposite:
Les Desmoiselles d'Avignon, 1907 (Museum of Modern Art, New York) Often described as the first true twentieth-century painting, this work contravened all established rules of Renaissance art and was unpopular in the extreme when it was first viewed by Picasso's friends and admirers.

Picasso's Cubist paintings, arguably the most revolutionary ever produced by any artist, emerged in the spring of 1907, while he was still only in his twenties. With one dramatic work, Picasso demolished all existing conventions of Western art, unleashing a storm of protest, inviting upon himself a charge of heresy decreed by a public recoiling in horror from the brutal violation of the artist's traditional role.

Even Picasso's most devoted and adventurous admirers reacted with shock and disbelief at his first Cubist painting, *Les Demoiselles d'Avignon*. Matisse accused him of making a deliberate mockery of modern art; Max Jacob and Guillaume Apollinaire could see nothing of value in the picture. Ambroise Vollard refused to buy the new canvases and even Georges Braque accused the artist of 'drinking petrol in the hope of spitting fire'. Scarcely a single person in Paris praised Picasso's new experimental art. Temporarily defeated and forlorn, he rolled up the canvas and buried it among the vast number of other paintings crammed into his small studio. It was only reproduced for the first time in 1925, in the July edition of *The Surrealist Revolution*. In 1937, thirty years after its creation, it was finally exhibited at the Paris International Exhibition, to a far more receptive public. Early sketches reveal that the central figure was at first a sailor and the second male was a student holding a skull in his hand as he entered to the left of the picture. Both of these figures were eventually removed in favour of an all-female portrait.

Les Demoiselles d'Avignon was an astounding innovation, effectively ending the long domination of Renaissance-style art. Picasso made at least thirty sketches in pencil, charcoal, watercolour, pastel and oil before deciding on the final composition. The differences between this painting and those of his Rose Period are enormous; the pale pink shades alone are reminiscent of this earlier work. For a good many months he had been moving steadily towards a more abstract art, stripped of sentimental appeal. He had reached a point where he needed to destroy the image people had of him as a painter. The destruction manifested itself in his dissection of the human form, followed by its re-assembly into something unexpected, yet eminently possible. The first version of the *Les Demoiselles d'Avignon* originally contained seven figures, two men and five women. Picasso spurned the practice of giving names to his paintings; this picture was christened by his friends after a notorious brothel area in the city. He took a giant, courageous step forward, ignoring conventional perspective and the rational position of his figures in space. He was no longer interested in struggling to achieve a three-dimensional illusion on the canvas, but began to tamper generously with the appearance of natural forms, exploring his conviction that underneath the visible

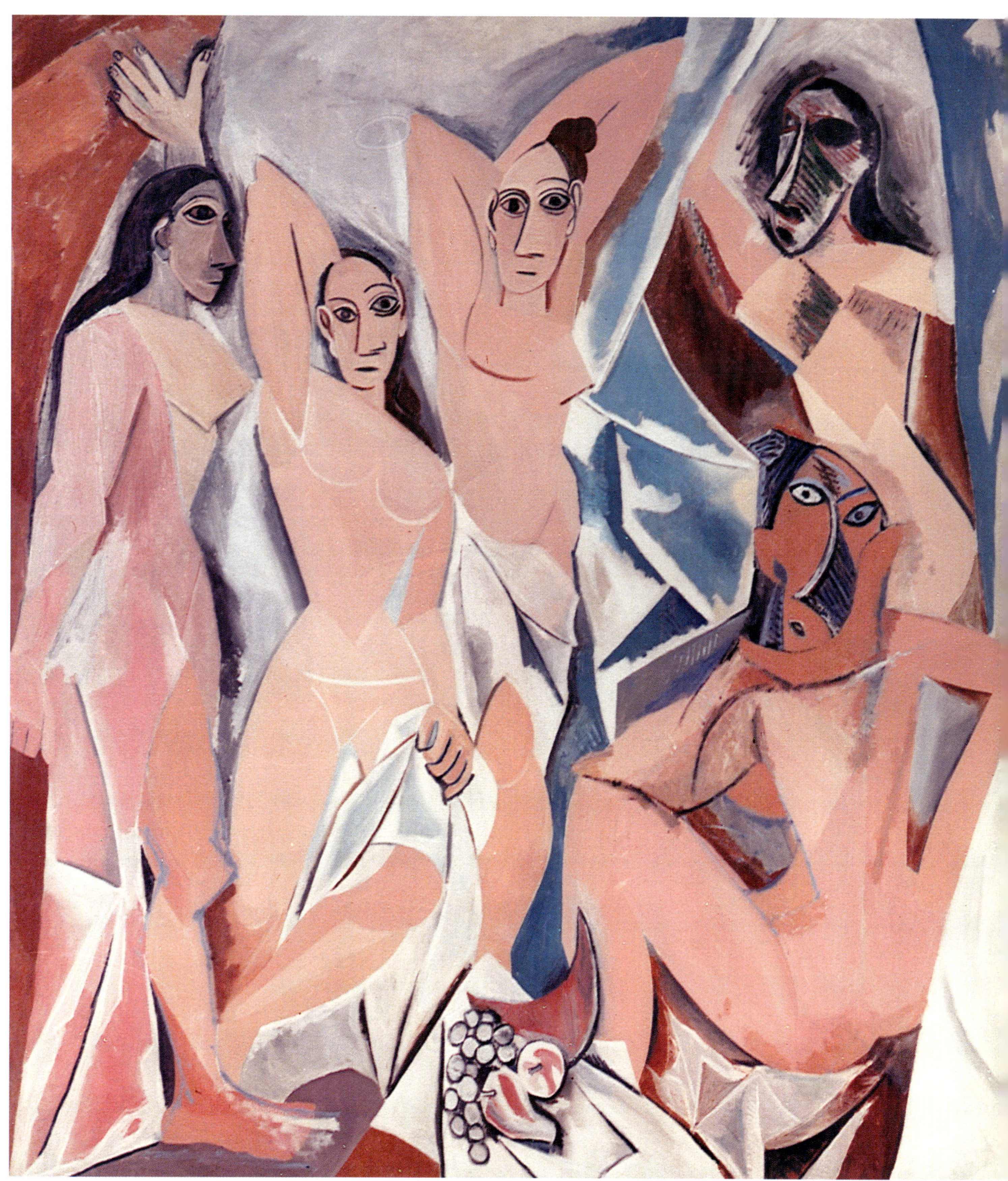

existed numerous other visible possibilities. He wanted to examine the 'possibly visible' in his art.

Les Demoiselles d'Avignon refuses to honour the myth of feminine beauty. In this painting, Picasso asks us to abandon all preconceived ideas of form, to disregard natural representation, to examine the fragments that make up his naked females as self-sufficient elements in themselves. The perspective is entirely flat and the manner in which he paints his nudes challenges all traditional principles of anatomy. A comparison with Ingres' *The Turkish Bath*, which Picasso undoubtedly used as a source, emphasizes this challenge very forcefully. The gentle contours of Ingres' females have disappeared, the sensual beauty is entirely replaced. Picasso's painting is without narrative, he uses style alone to unite his large number of figures. His women are an intimidating construction of diverse geometrical planes, ovoid shapes and grotesque distortions. He invites us to view every aspect of the human form simultaneously, following Cézanne's doctrine that truth has no bounding lines, but exists as a presence emerging from all different aspects united together.

The savage, deformed heads reveal eyes placed on different levels and noses painted in profile on forward-looking faces. Picasso displays an incredible economy of means in the facial features, delineated by broad, angular, black lines, painted with single, sweeping strokes of the brush. Bodies and heads are divided up into angular wedges of flesh. Open areas are filled in with colour and there is very little shaping in these spaces. There are no subtle variations of light and darkness either to soften the ungainly shapes of the women's bodies. Two of the five figures have monster heads, clearly derivative of African tribal masks, while the remaining three figures project the influence of Iberian sculpture. Both the face and back are simultaneously visible on the crouching nude to the lower right of the painting. The woman above her has the face of a canine, her snout-like lower jaw is slashed with ritual markings, her body fragmented into a diverse assortment of incompatible, irregular shapes.

> *Cubism is no different from any other school of painting. The same principles and the same elements are common to all. The fact that for a long time Cubism has not been understood and that even today there are people who cannot see anything in it, means nothing. I do not read English, and an English book is a blank book to me. This does not mean that the English language does not exist, and why should I blame anyone but myself if I cannot understand what I know nothing about?*

Picasso uttered these words long after Cubism had been established as a formidable art movement. Its recognition as such however,

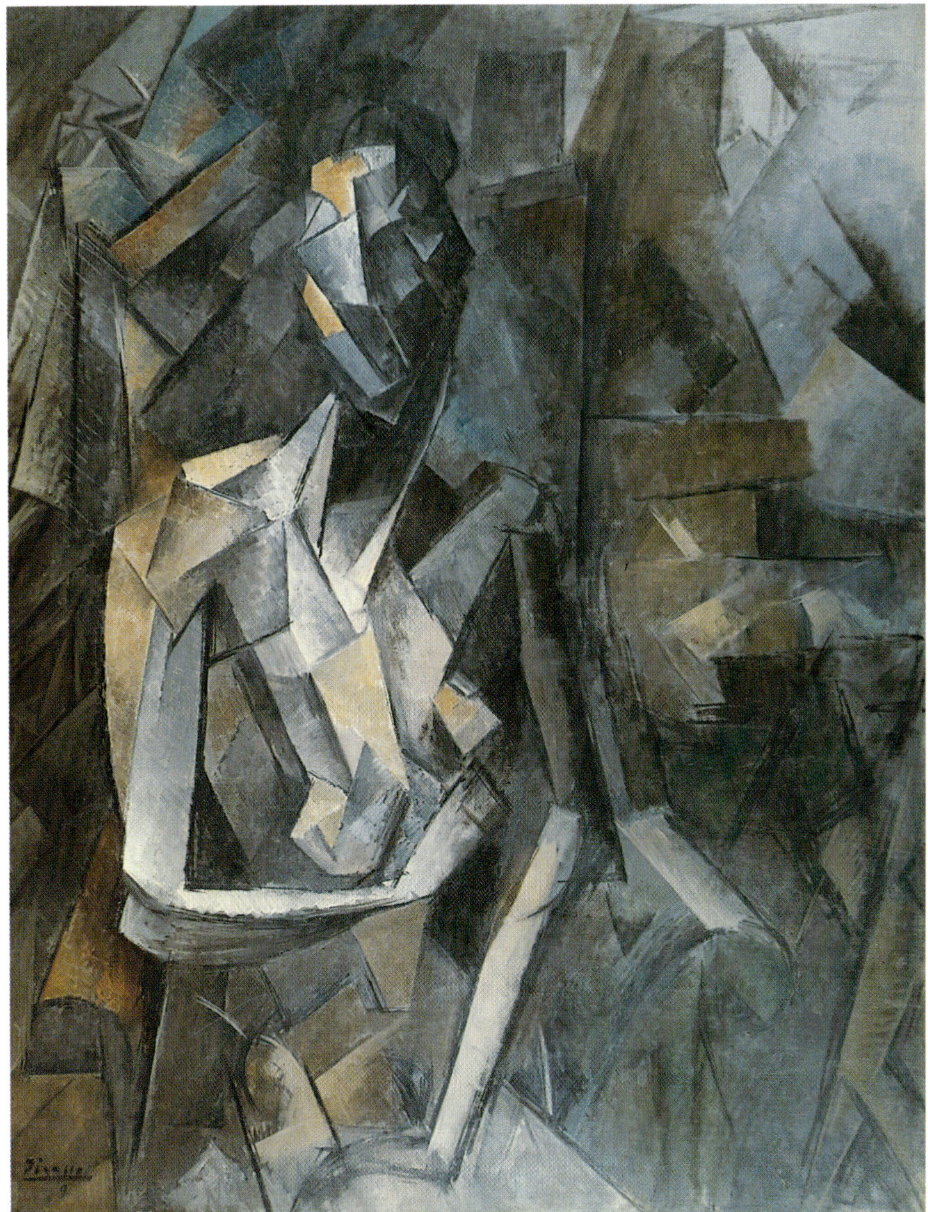

Seated Nude **(Tate Gallery, London)**
Painted in the winter of 1909 to 1910, Picasso's nude demonstrates the pronounced move towards a more abstract style of Cubist art with its use of greys, dull browns, or monochrome.

demanded a tremendous amount of self-belief and perseverance on the part of its creator. Picasso was well aware that he could not retreat into the past and take up again a style of painting which had ceased to inspire him in any way. He had one faithful supporter at this time of crisis, a fledgling art dealer named Daniel Henry Kahnweiler, who was a friend of the wealthy German art critic and collector, Wilhelm Uhde. Kahnweiler's response to *Les Demoiselles d'Avignon* was highly enthusiastic. He purchased all of Picasso's sketches for the piece and would have bought the painting itself, but could not afford it. Kahnweiler's portrait was one of the outstanding works Picasso painted in the Cubist style some years later.

Although the Frenchman, Georges Braque, was at first disdainful of Picasso's Cubist masterpiece, he too became haunted by the revolu-

Cubist Portrait of Braque **(Private Collection)** Picasso painted many of his best Cubist portraits during 1910. Braque is still recognizable from this picture, although Picasso soon replaced identifiable features with very basic 'keys' to the sitter's identity, buried in a canvas of 'super-imposed' planes.

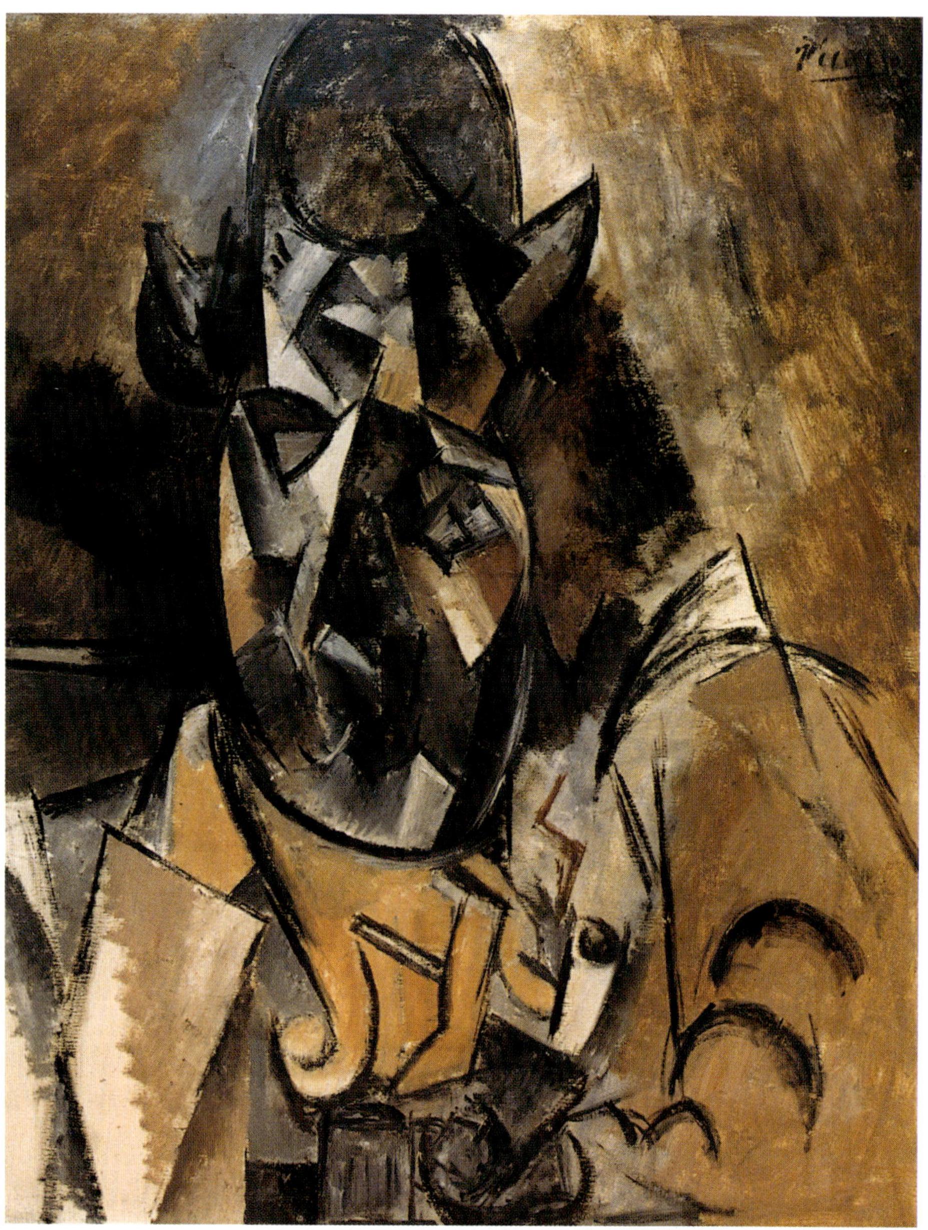

tionary power of the work. He believed, however, that it was 'a mistake to imitate what one wants to create' and before collaborating with Picasso on many of the subsequent Cubist works, he first established his own autonomy as an artist. Braque's *Grand Nu* was painted in December 1907, after seeing Picasso's *Les Desmoiselles d'Avignon.* It shares some of Picasso's innovations, including the simultaneous showing of the face and back and the same bulky representation of form, but it is also a more lyrical expression of the artist's skill. Braque always worked with Picasso as an equal. It was pure coincidence that they both began to explore problems of form and perspective, as Cézanne had done before them, through landscape painting. The two men returned from their respective summer vacations of 1908 with strikingly similar paintings. It was at this point that they decided to work together. They became intimate friends in spite of artistic rivalry. Braque admitted that they were like climbers joined together by a rope, each one hoisting the other up. Eventually their relationship resembled a form of marriage. They frequently omitted to sign their canvases, as evidence of their dedication to a mutual goal. It was Matisse, according to one story, who gave the new movement its name. He observed that Braque's work was full of *'petits cubes'*. The collaborative output of Braque and Picasso was repeatedly described as 'Cubist' and the name took hold within a relatively short time.

The first phase of the new movement, known as 'Analytical Cubism', lasted until 1912. It was characterized by the geometrical representation of familiar objects, such as bottles, glasses of wine, musical instruments, portraits and landscapes, painted in subdued colours, usually greys, browns, muddy greens and ochres. Colour was at this stage considered a distraction to the analysis of form. In an effort to combat the problem of reflecting a three-dimensional world on a two-dimensional canvas, Cubism demanded a view of reality from all angles at the same time. The composition of a picture was no longer a simple matter of one central perspective. The viewer was forced to look everywhere at once in order to interpret and fully appreciate the image before him. Cubism took extreme liberties with nature and the visual world became severely fragmented as a result. Recognizable objects were painted in an increasingly abstract and disjointed manner by the end of this analytical period.

In the summer of 1909, Picasso stayed at Horta de Ebro, the village where he had spent time with his friend, Pallares, some ten years earlier. The austere Spanish scenery did not lend itself to traditional landscape painting, but it readily fulfilled the requirements of the Cubist artist. Picasso painted his first series of truly Cubist pictures of the Spanish countryside, now experimenting with spacial distances and abandoning detail in favour of block or wedge-shaped representations. Fernande Olivier was also the subject of two very powerful Cubist pieces at this time. The sculpture *Woman's Head,* cast in bronze, was one of Picasso's earliest in this style, consisting of jagged planes modelled together to produce a face closely resembling that of his mistress. It demonstrates Picasso's genius in overcoming the problems of transferring a new art, essentially developed for two-dimensional pictures, to the three dimensions of sculpture. His *Portrait of Fernande* in oil is a parallel two-dimensional creation, which although unflattering, does not conceal the personality of its subject.

Between 1909 and 1913, portraits and still-lifes were some of Picasso's main themes. The early Cubist still-life, *Fruit Dish,* set a precedent in its failure to deliver a traditional artist's impression of looking through a window at a carefully arranged scene. Picasso stripped his objects to their basic forms and the table on which these objects rested was tilted forward in the extreme, denying the viewer a comfortable three-dimensional illusion. Many of his best Cubist portraits were painted in 1910, leaning more and more towards abstraction, including those of Ambroise Vollard, Georges Braque, Wilhelm Uhde and Daniel-Henry Kahnweiler. Uhde, Vollard and Braque can be easily identified from their portraits. Picasso's drawing overrules the Cubist preoccupation with superimposed planes. Vollard's bearded face and heavy eyelids, for example, remain visible in spite of the painting's extremely complex structure and almost monochrome colouring. The later portrait of Kahnweiler, on the other hand, which Picasso completed in the autumn, provides only 'keys' to help establish the sitter's identity – Kahnweiler's gold watch-chain, his nose and hands, his distinctively parted black hair. Picasso justified this move towards abstraction with the following statement some years later:

> *Braque always used to say that the only thing which really mattered in painting was the intention. And that is true. What matters is what you do. That is the most important thing. And what was particularly important about Cubism was what you wanted to do, your intention. And you cannot paint that.*

Cubism had successfully infiltrated the artistic circles of Paris by the spring of 1911. Criticism had abated and many of Picasso's fellow artists had assimilated the movement's principles and practical techniques in their art. Marcel Duchamp and Piet Mondrian had emerged as gifted artists in their own right, unequivocally inspired by the Cubist movement. The works of Braque and Picasso were displayed at Kahnweiler's small gallery and the paintings now sold extremely well.

Their period of successful collaboration was gradually coming to an end, however. The two men decided to spend the summer of 1911 on holiday together and they travelled to Céret, in the eastern Pyrénées. Picasso had again entered a period of acute restlessness which would not subside. He was unhappy that the balance between naturalism and abstraction in his work had been upset and he began to lose interest in predominantly abstract pictures. His allegiance to the movement's abstract orientation survived the summer, nonetheless. During their stay in Céret, Picasso and Braque produced works that were virtually identical in subject matter and method. Braque painted his *Man with a Guitar* at this time, which is difficult to tell apart from Picasso's *Accordionist*. Both are portraits of seated musicians but, in each case, the musical instruments and also the bodies of the players are barely discernible. Scroll patterns suggest the arms of

Portrait of D.H. Kahnweiler, **1910 (Chicago Art Institute)** Kahnweiler became one of Picasso's most important supporters at a time when Cubism was being rejected by even the most enterprising of Picasso's friends. This portrait, painted during the late 'Analytical Period', fully embraces the movement's journey towards abstraction.

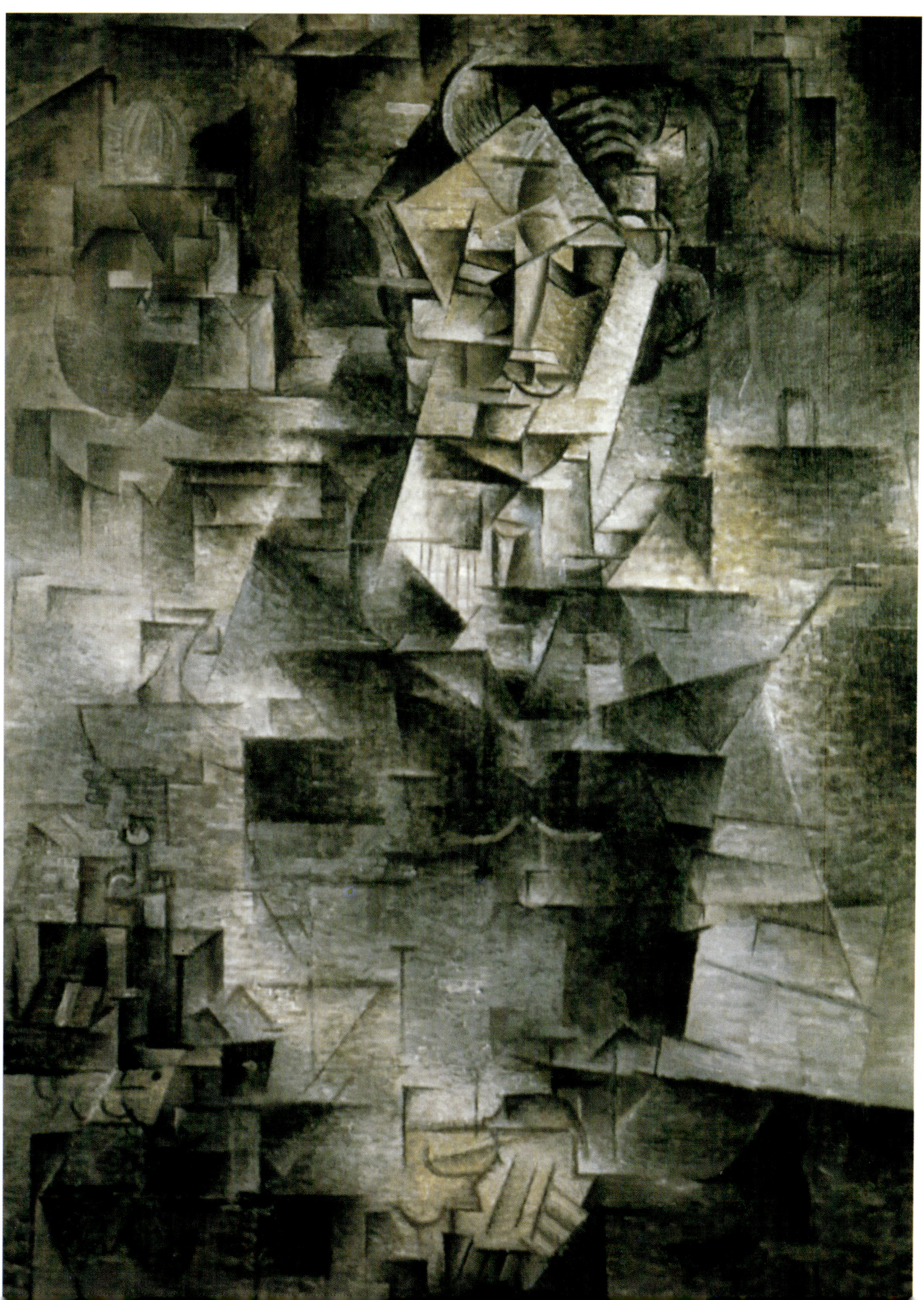

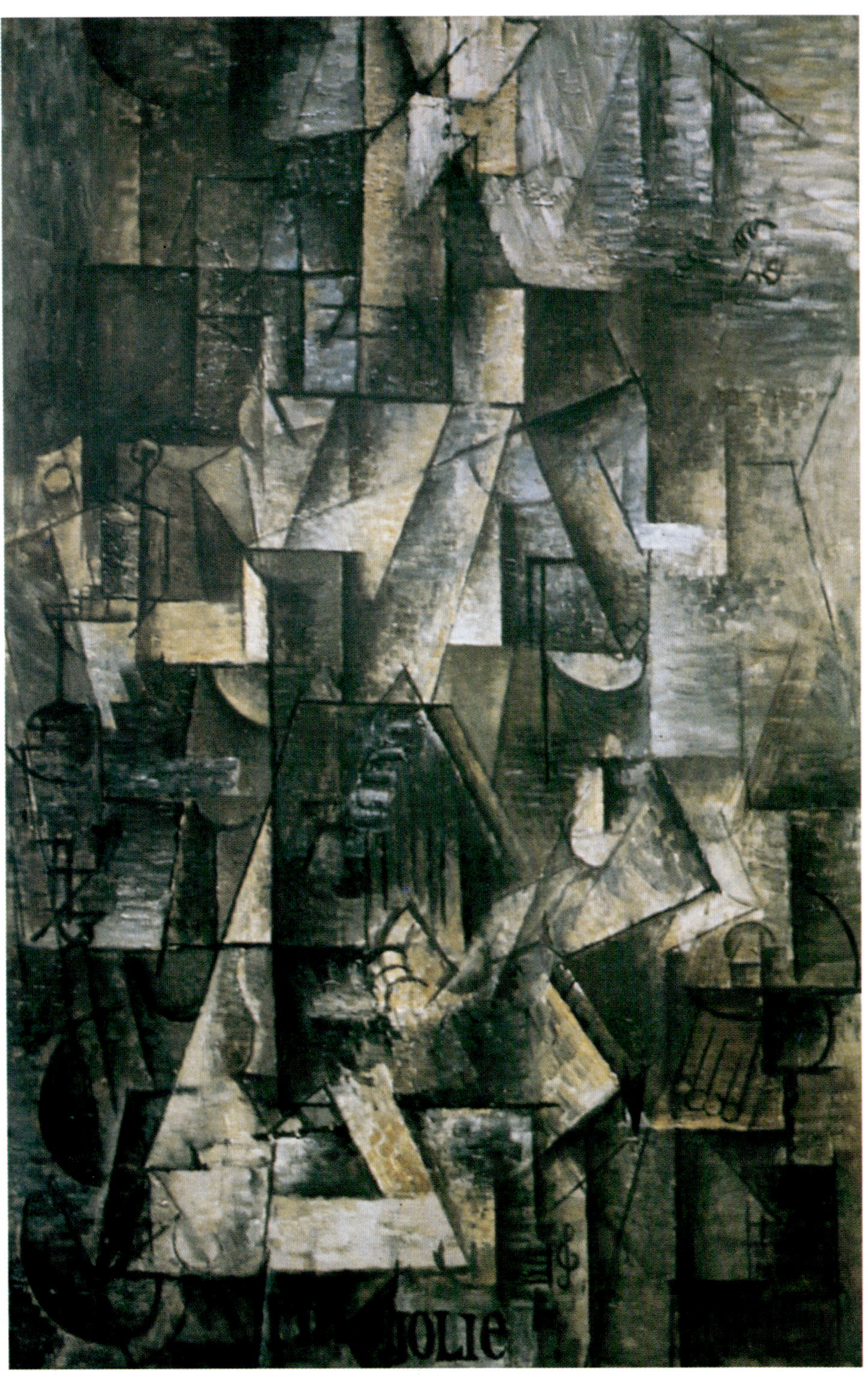

Ma Jolie, **1911–12 (Museum of Modern Art, New York)** Fernande Olivier reputedly walked out on Picasso in 1911 after a bitter row, carrying with her about eleven francs and forty bottles of perfume. Picasso painted this picture for his new mistress 'Eva'. His use of printed letters on the canvas was an attempt to reintroduce a sense of reality into his art.

chairs in both pictures and the instruments themselves are radically simplified. In Picasso's painting, the accordion is represented by a number of pleats and by some of the instrument's keys. In Braque's painting, the guitar is no more than a few frets, indicated by a row of parallel lines.

While in Céret, Picasso began to investigate a means by which he might add animation to his art. In conjunction with Braque, he soon discovered and employed certain elements in his paintings which he considered to have sufficient expressive value to combat the excessively abstract nature of his work. The first of Picasso's new canvases contained printed or stencilled letters in an attempt to restore some semblance of reality and identity to his paintings. The decline of 'Analytical Cubism' was prompted by this practice. A second phase had been entered, and a third important individual was added to the movement. In the company of Spanish-born artist, Juan Gris, Braque and Picasso embraced a new form of Cubism, which was rapidly christened 'Synthetic Cubism'.

By the time Picasso returned to Paris at the end of the summer of 1911, his relationship with Fernande had begun to show obvious signs of disintegration. He would frequently go out in the evening leaving her behind and had begun to flirt openly with other women. By 1912, a new female had entered his life, a woman named Marcelle Humbert whom he affectionately referred to as Eva. Picasso fell deeply in love and, for a time, remained blissfully happy. He began to write Eva's name on his pictures. She was his inspiration for two paintings from this period containing the words, 'J'aime Eva', and she also inspired the painting *Ma Jolie*.

It was not long before Picasso employed other examples of 'real' detail in his work, never before used by any artist on a canvas. By the end of 1911, he had moved on to using fragments of newspaper, wood, marble and even sand. The most famous example of this kind of painting, using the technique known as 'Papier collé' or 'collages', was produced in the spring of 1912, and is entitled *Still Life with Cane Chair*. Picasso was intent on exploring the relationship between reality and illusion in his collages, introducing increasingly complex juxtapositions. He pasted a piece of oil cloth on to his canvas, printed to look like chair caning. At the same time, he developed a brushstroke imitating the effect of the glued object, creating other areas made to look like collage, so that it was almost impossible to differentiate between the two. He framed his painting with a length of rope, presenting the illusion of a gilded frame. Cubism was now placing less and less emphasis on the distortion of form. Braque, Picasso and Gris began to paint in brighter colours and the objects represented became easily recognizable again. Analysis had made room for a more subjective interpretation of form.

Several dramatic changes occurred in Picasso's life with the outbreak of the First World War. The most immediate and significant effect of the war was the termination of his partnership with Braque, who joined the French army and departed for the front. The two never again collaborated together, but adopted different artistic directions, Braque continuing to adhere to the formal unity of Cubism, Picasso reverting to a more naturalistic style of art. Many more of

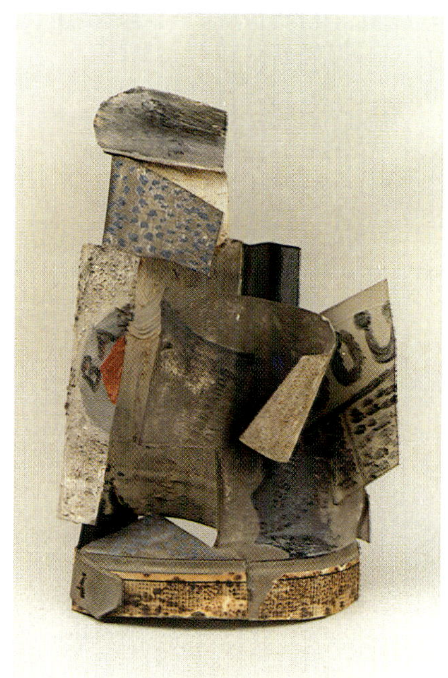

Bass Bottle and Newspaper, **1914 (Musée Picasso, Paris)** Picasso pioneered the collage effect, together with Georges Braque. He took it to extremes, employing wood, marble, fabric, newspaper and even sand in the production of his collages.

Harlequin with a Guitar, **1918 (Private Collection)** Picasso's work, at this period was moving steadily towards a more realistic representation of form. Here, his harlequin is closer to his Rose Period figures than any Cubist representation.

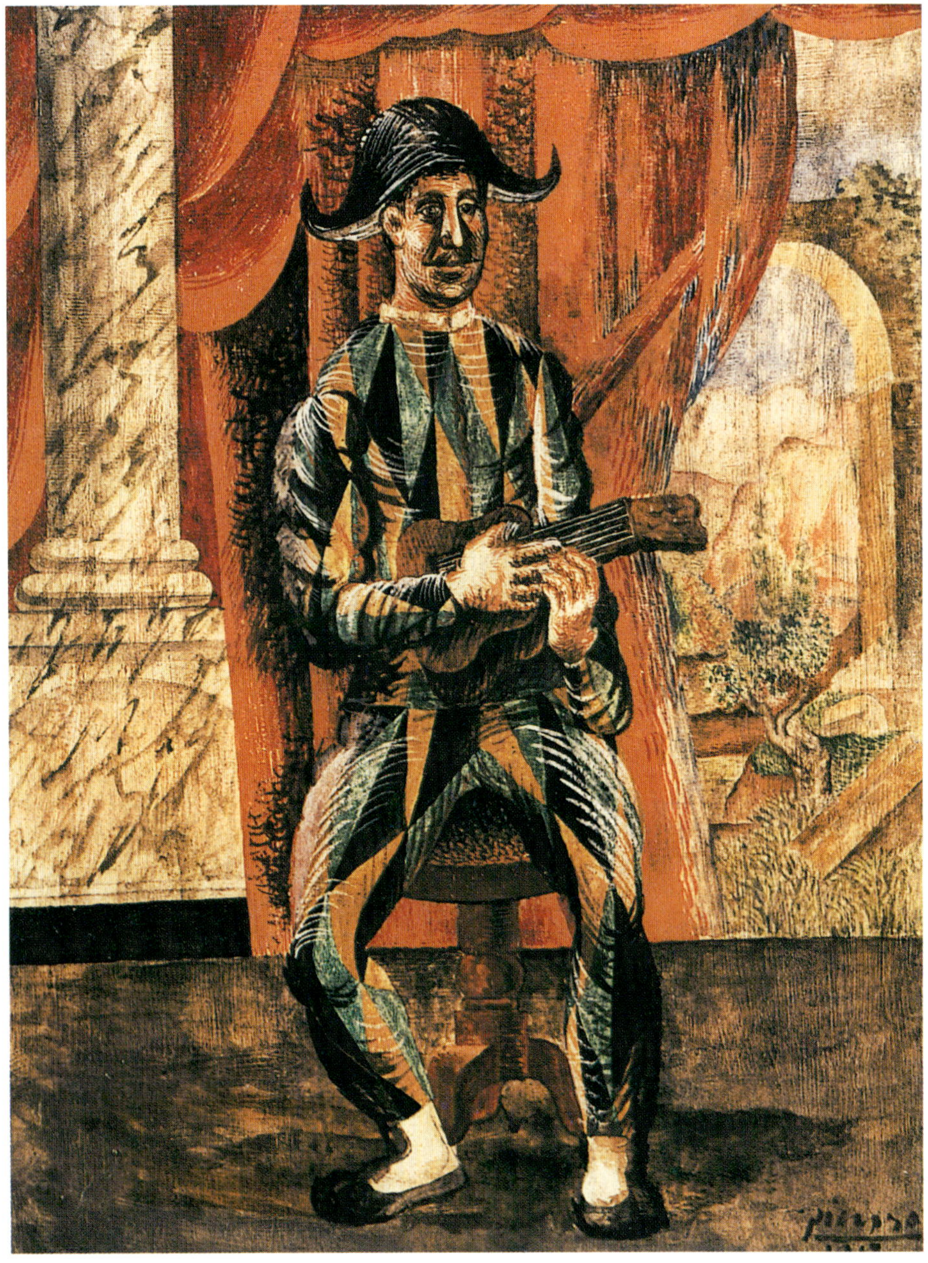

Opposite:
Madame Picasso, **1920 (Metropolitan Museum, New York)** Picasso's wife, Olga Khokhlova, was a member of the Ballet Russes and they met when he was commissioned to design the sets and costumes for the ballet. This portrait of her stems from the period when he had begun to paint and draw the human figure realistically and to introduce a delicate, lyrical quality into his work.

Picasso's friends were scattered during the war. Picasso's father also died at this time and Eva became acutely ill. To the dismay of Cubist hard-liners, Picasso began to journey away from an art which for years had confined him to the portrayal of mere objects. He could no longer satisfy himself in a world limited to his studio and a selection of everyday things. His naturalistic drawings of Vollard and Max Jacob at this time appear to be imitating Ingres in their brilliantly executed style of Neoclassicism. Jean-Auguste Ingres was a leading exponent of the movement which sprung up among artists in the middle of the eighteenth century. True Neoclassicists sought to reform society through an art which revived ancient standards of morality and idealism. Picasso's portraits caused a sensation.

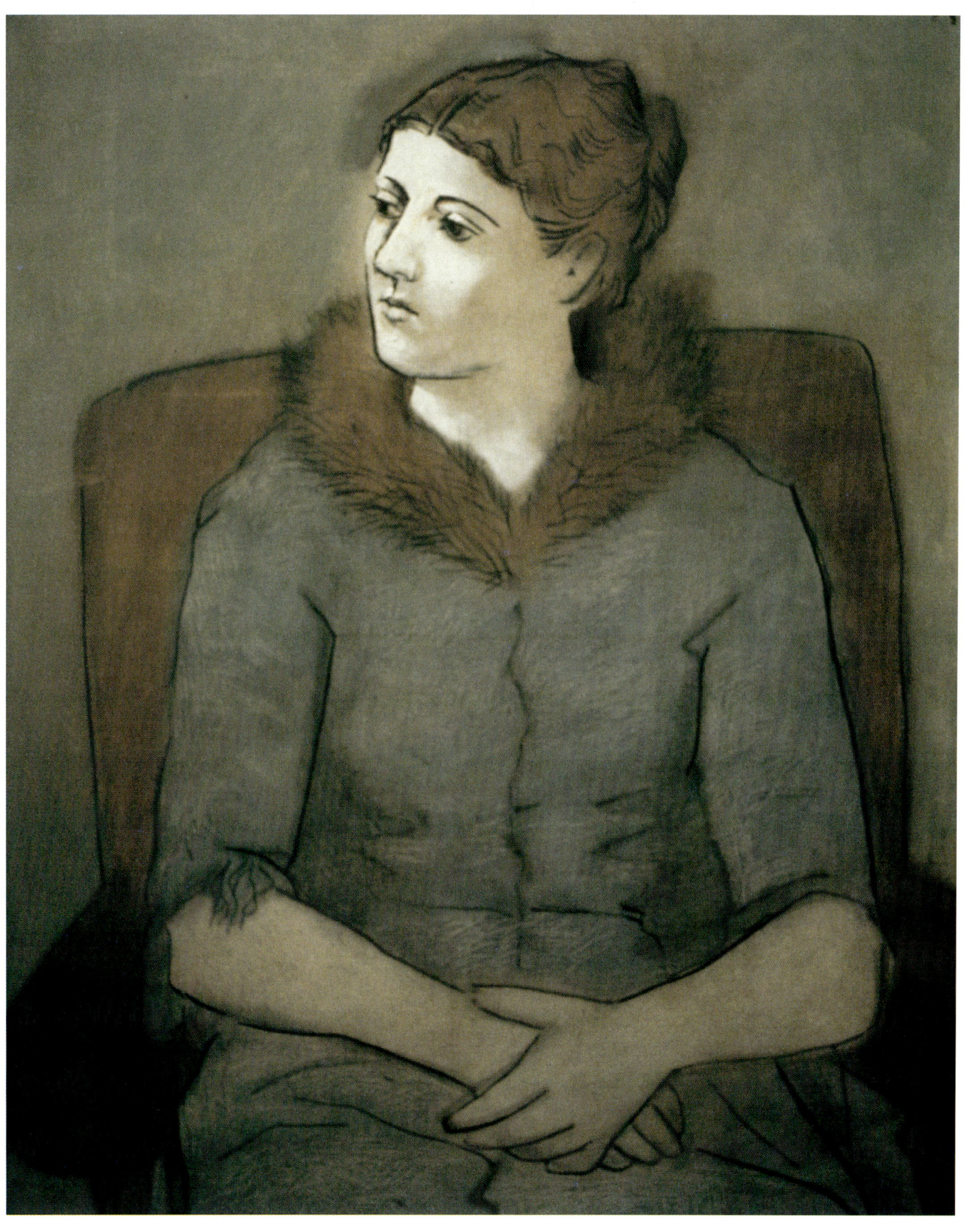

The Pipes of Pan, **1920 (Musée Picasso, Paris)** Picasso was deeply influenced by the sculptural and architectural treasures of Rome when he visited the city in 1917. His art, after he had finished working with the Ballet Russes, strongly reflected classical Roman influences.

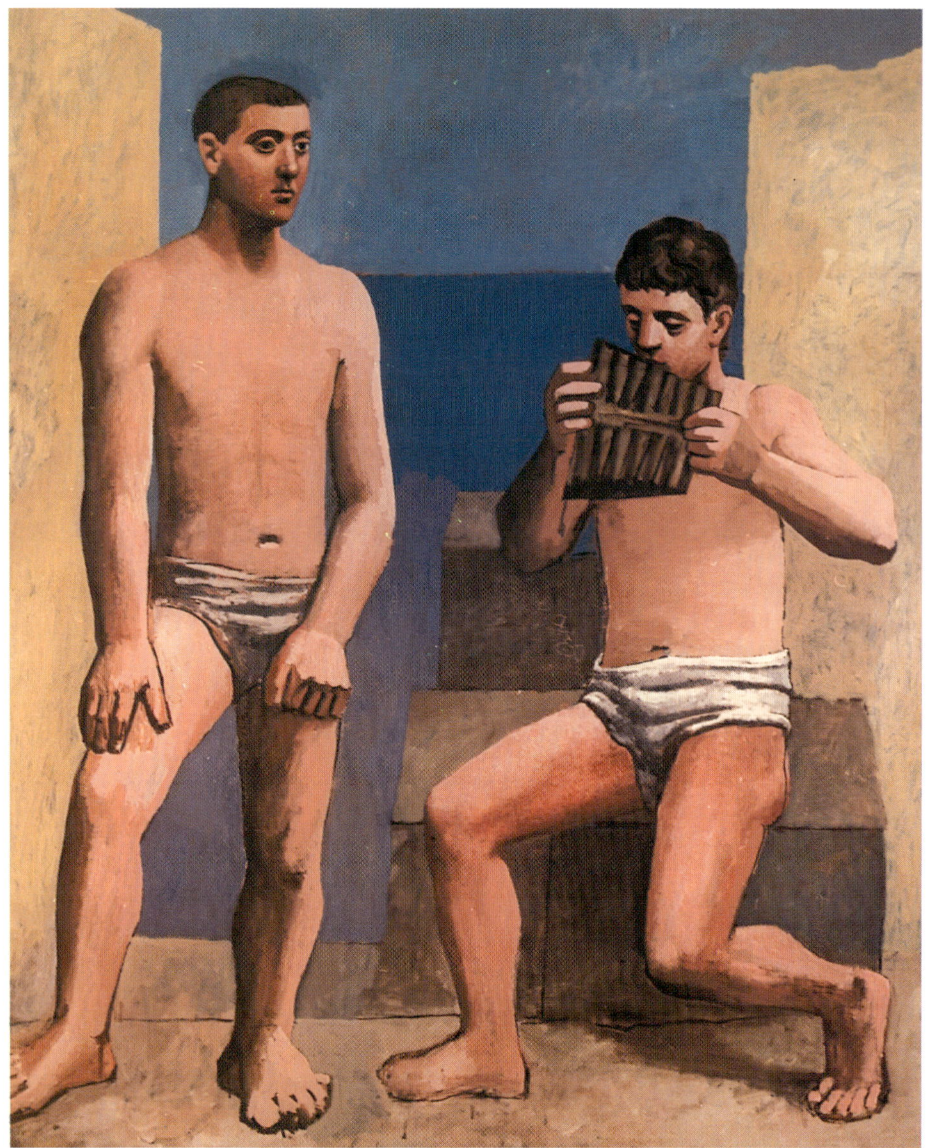

Adherents of Cubism were scandalized by them and Picasso was rather unfairly criticized for turning his back on the movement he had himself created without, it seemed, any qualms.

Eva died in the winter of 1915–16 and Picasso moved out of Paris, now occupied by the Germans, to the suburb of Montrouge, three miles from the city. It was here that he met Eric Satie, a man fifteen years his senior, who had successfully established himself as an avant-garde composer. Satie was working on the music for a new ballet, with libretto written by the nascent playwright, Jean Cocteau. Although he continued to paint some works in the Cubist style, Picasso was desperately searching for a new outlet for his art and was also eager to escape the painful memories of Eva's death. Satie had little difficulty persuading him to become involved with the Ballet Russes. Picasso was invited to design the sets and costumes and, in February 1917, he travelled to Rome to attend the rehearsals of the company's forthcoming production of *Parade.* Cocteau's subject matter, given a burlesque treatment, was the circus. Picasso was in familiar territory and the back-cloth he designed for the event featured harlequins, musicans and performers, painted in fresh and lively colours, calling to mind the best work of his Rose Period.

The ballet opened in May, but was not at all well received. It was too unconventional and modern for its Parisian audience, accustomed to the elegant, classical beauty of dance performance. Cocteau had removed all traces of romance and sentiment from his drama; Satie had produced a musical score which included the use of typewriters and Morse signals. Picasso benefited from his experience with the ballet in two ways, however. His art had taken a different direction, newly inspired by the majestic, lyrical power of Rome's Imperial architecture and the city's vast collection of artistic masterpieces. He also met Olga Khokhlova, a dancer with the Ballet Russes, who returned with Picasso to Paris and accepted his rather sudden invitation to marry.

Olga and Picasso moved to an expensive apartment off the Champs Elysées. The ballet's lack of success served only to increase the artist's popularity and fame. His lifestyle changed from bohemian to bourgeois and his paintings and sculpture began to reflect not only the grandeur of Rome's majestic art, but also a sense of inner calm and maturity. In much of his work, he reverted to drawing the human figure in a more realistic fashion and his great Neoclassical master-pieces were produced at this time. He completed several portraits of Olga which emphasized her classical beauty, in marked contrast to the Cubist portraits of Fernande. He was invited to work with the ballet for a second time in 1919, and the production, *The Three-Cornered Hat,* was a spectacular success on this occasion. He was undoubtedly revitalized by his sense of achievement and painted energetically in a whole variety of styles. He had not forgotten Cubism, however, in spite of the pronounced 'classical' slant now emerging.

He painted *Seated Woman, Sleeping Peasants* and *Women Running on a Beach* before the end of 1922. The last of these three paintings depicts the human body in a gloriously robust and muscular aspect; monumental in stature, yet graceful like the ballet. The two fleshy women may well have been inspired by Olga's pregnancy – their son Paolo was born in February 1921. By 1923, Picasso's classical style had reached a level of outstanding perfection. He painted *Les Amants* and also *The Pipes of Pan,* which some consider the most important picture of this period. It radiates an idyllic atmosphere of Roman antiquity, the figures are statuesque and tranquil, no longer distorted or grotesque. Paolo, too, became the subject of many of Picasso's finest paintings at this time. *Paul as Harlequin,* painted in 1924, was one of Picasso's favourite portraits of his son. He also re-introduced the mother and child theme to his work at this time.

In the midst of his 'classical' phase, Picasso managed to produce two remarkable Cubist paintings. The large canvases, each measuring over six square feet, were completed in 1921. Each of the paintings, entitled *Three Musicians*, depicts a monk, a harlequin and a pierrot, painted in the vivid colours of Synthetic Cubism. The fragmented forms, having undergone a process of careful, geometric analysis, are skilfully re-assembled to produce a unified creative whole. These were Picasso's last paintings in a truly Cubist style. The movement began to decline after this date. In 1921, the French government decided to auction the contents of the German-born Kahnweiler's gallery to the public and many Cubist paintings were sold for next to nothing.

For a number of years, Picasso remained remote from the wide-spread unrest of post-war European society. The discordant social atmosphere permeated the art world and resulted in movements such as Nihilism, which denied all established values, and Dadaism, which criticized all art forms, offering no favourable substitute. Surrealism was born at this time, influenced by Sigmund Freud's startling explorations of the human psyche, and the movement sought to produce an art reflecting the turmoil of man's inner and outer world. Picasso's classical forms occupied him until 1925, at which point he again altered his style without warning and began to explore a sense of anxious nightmare through his art. The sudden change, nourished by the social atmosphere of disaffection, may have been abruptly triggered by the fact that after eight years, his marriage to Olga was in trouble. But other forces were also at work. Once again, Picasso felt his individuality was slowly slipping away from him. He was tired of a public who blindly applauded every single work emerging from his studio. The gentle figures he had been painting now gave way to an almost demonic representation of the human figure, especially the female form. He began to manipulate the body on canvas as never before, exploiting his heartfelt conviction that 'nature and art are two different things. Through art we express our conception of what nature is not'. His painting, *The Three Dancers*, heralded the beginning of this new, extraordinary phase. Closing the door firmly on his classical world, he displayed utter contempt for contemporary form, mercilessly ripping the human body apart, dislocating and distorting limbs, breasts and facial features to produce his most violent, metamorphic art to date.

Surrealists, including André Breton, took solace in Picasso's new style and *The Three Dancers* was chosen to illustrate Surrealist ideology, in particular, the belief that 'beauty must be convulsive, or cease to be'. Breton published *Les Demoiselles d'Avignon* in his reactionary magazine and Picasso was invited to exhibit at the first Surrealist Exhibition in Paris in 1925. He did not consider himself a Surrealist

Three Musicians, 1921 (**Philadelphia Museum of Art**) Although Picasso had ceased to immerse himself in Cubism, he would still abruptly revert to the style when it suited him, transferring his skill, without difficulty, from ancient to modern styles. He painted two large canvases at this time, both entitled *Three Musicians,* which many consider the apogee of Synthetic Cubism.

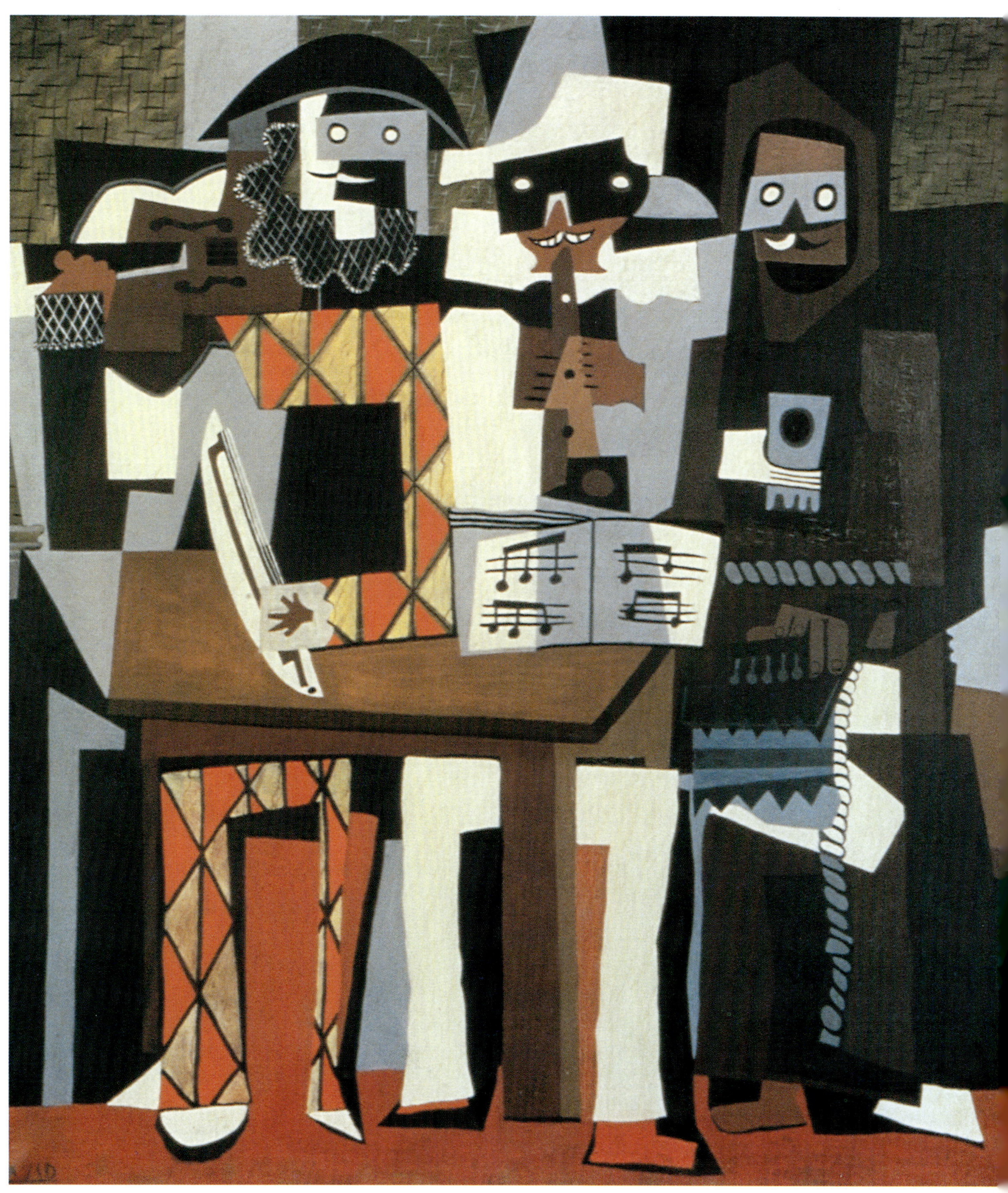

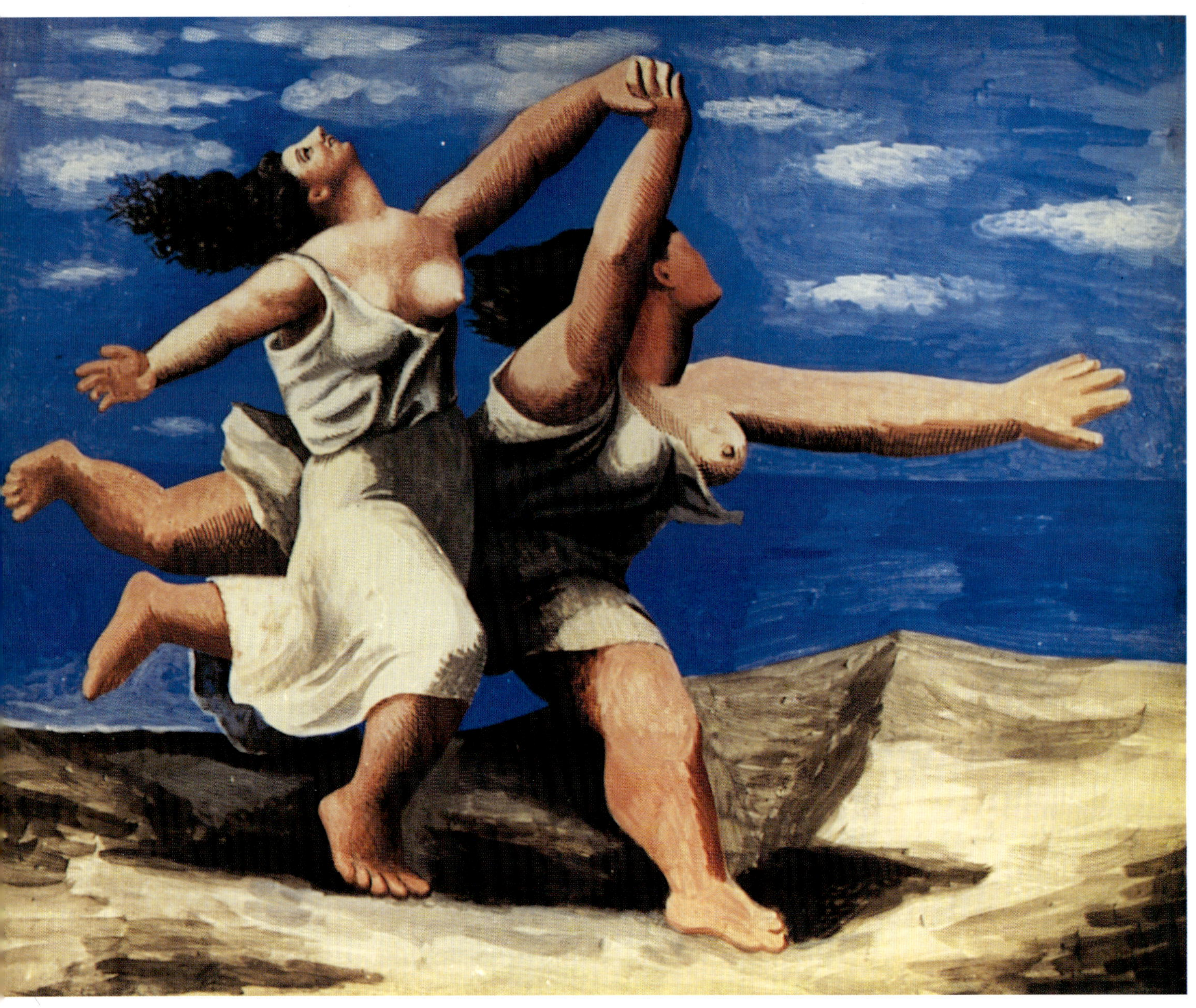

Women Running on the Beach, **1922 (Musée Picasso, Paris)** The diversity of Picasso's art is truly astounding, especially when one is left to consider the fact that only a year before he produced this classically inspired painting with its atmosphere of happy abandon, he painted two of his finest Cubist paintings ever, entirely bereft of similar emotion.

painter, however. The movement encouraged artists to practise introspection and although Picasso tended towards self-analysis in times of crisis, he was fundamentally a realist. He set out primarily to enrich the vocabulary of form and was never content to limit himself to any one style. The next five years were an intense period of bold experimentation. His destruction of the human figure gathered momentum and he produced such works as *Seated Woman* (1927), *Woman in an Armchair* (1929), and *Seated Bather* (1930). Picasso was not afraid of losing what had already been won and his successes only multiplied with each new risk taken.

The metamorphosis of the human form was an obsession which held his attention well into the early 1930s and its indulgence was not simply restricted to painting. After almost two decades, apart from a few Cubist experiments, Picasso, now in his fifties, began to devote himself to exploring the medium of sculpture with renewed vigour, recognizing it as the ultimate challenge of metamorphic art. The period from 1929 until 1933 witnessed his most intense output in this area. Until 1931, he collaborated with fellow-Spaniard, Julio Gonzalez, and, as had been the case with Braque, the two men introduced countless innovations to a field of art once dominated by traditional methods. Picasso rapidly abandoned conventional materials, replacing them with a whole host of scrap-yard objects, including screws, wheels, hinges, bolts and kitchen utensils, such as colanders and sieves. He also employed new techniques, producing a collage effect in his sculpture, not unlike the highly original paintings of his period of Synthetic Cubism. After 1931, once he had satisfied his passion for iron constructions, he began to use clay and plaster, producing a series of *Women's Heads* featuring remarkable distortions of the nose, made to resemble the trunks of elephants.

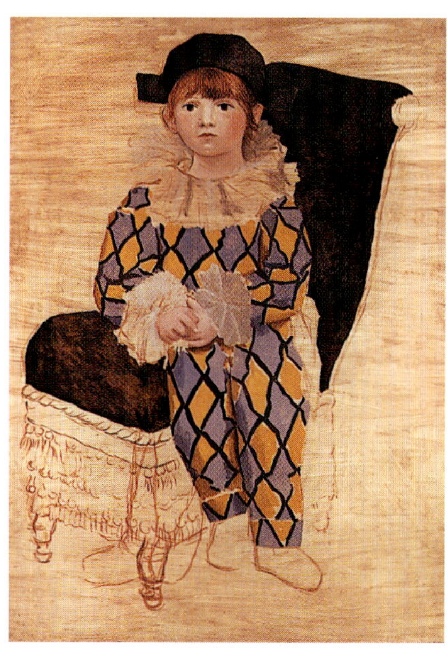

Paul as Harlequin, **1924 (Musée Picasso, Paris)** Picasso loved children dearly and was always described as a kind, attentive parent. Paolo, his first child, was born to his Russian wife, Olga, in February 1921. Inevitably, his son became a favourite subject for the artist.

Although it was proving very difficult, Picasso weathered his relationship with Olga for almost fourteen years. He believed his wife had no interest in his work, and that she only appreciated him for the social advantages his celebrity status offered. He sought an outlet from this estranged relationship and found it in Marie-Thérèse Walter, a woman half his age, whom he met in 1927 outside a Paris department store. As their relationship became more settled, Picasso's canvases were transformed by a new wave of creativity. Marie-Thérèse was everything Olga could never be – young, blonde, curvaceous, eager and good-humoured. Picasso's vengeful attack on the female figure was superseded by a lover's appreciation of his new mistress and she became the subject of a whole series of paintings, sculptures and etchings which first emerged in the winter of 1931.

Picasso's paintings of Marie-Thérèse pay generous tribute to her youthful beauty and vulnerability. The torment of his earlier work now disappeared and he concentrated instead on presenting a relaxed, sensual atmosphere. In many of the earlier paintings, Marie-Thérèse is seated, or sleeping, her blonde head resting on her arms, her lips full and parted, her voluptuous figure captured in an erotically inviting pose. *Girl Before a Mirror,* and *The Dream,* both painted in 1932, were two of Picasso's most impressive portraits of his young mistress and she also featured in his sculptures at this time. He made a number of plaster studies of her body and her head, eventually cast in bronze, progressing from a classical to a metamorphic style, where he concentrated heavily on distorting form, so that his subject matter was altered dramatically from the anticipated original structure and composition. Later paintings of Marie-Thérèse also reflect this progression: *Woman with a Flower,* portrays her in the distorted and deformed manner of Surrealism, *Interior with a Girl Drawing,* painted in 1935, shows a

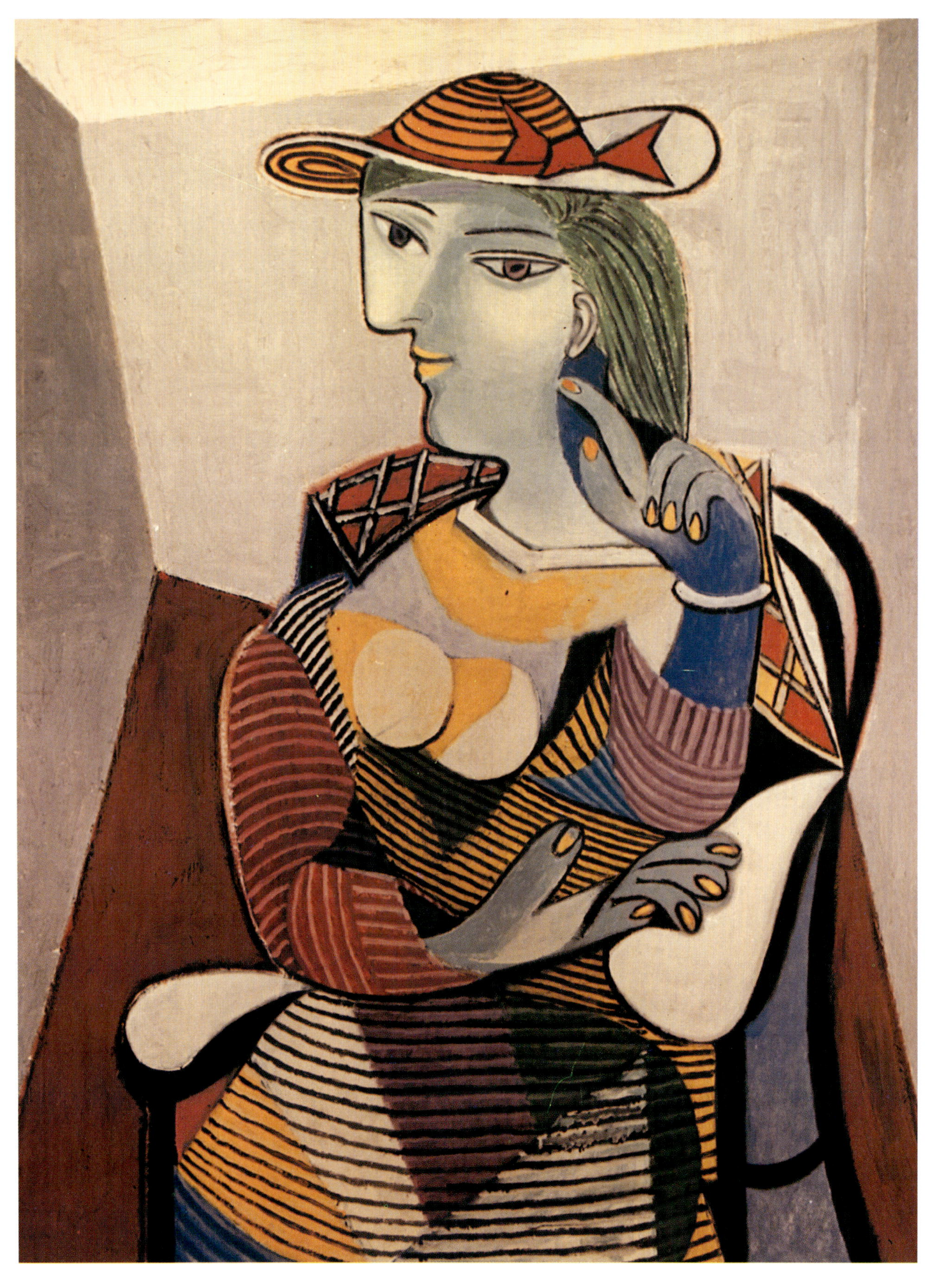

frontal view of the face which includes its profile, recalling his earlier Cubist art. Picasso's greatest tribute to Marie-Thérèse, however, was a series of etchings, entitled *The Sculptor's Studio,* which he completed in 1934. There were forty-six plates in the collection, featuring a bearded sculptor and his model, obviously involved in an intimate, loving relationship. The figures, never failing to make some form of physical contact, were drawn in a Neoclassical style.

At the age of fifty-two, Picasso was in his prime. He had fallen in love with a woman who inspired perhaps his most engaging art ever; he was a very wealthy man; he had developed an artistic language of his own and achieved the status of a modern deity. Yet within a year, he was wretched again, consumed by loneliness and admitting to a close circle of friends, that he had fallen into a deep depression and was going through one of the worst periods of his life.

In 1935, Picasso decided to remain in Paris for the summer, his first in over thirty years. He spent his time wrangling over the details of his separation from his wife. Lawyers had become involved in arranging adequate financial settlement for Olga. The divorce proceedings came to nothing however, since Spain did not allow divorce and Picasso refused to give up his citizenship. At the same time, Marie-Thérèse had given birth to Picasso's daughter, Maya, and had arrived in Paris to spend time with him. He visited her frequently, but was still unbearably despondent. Finally, he wrote to his close friend, Jaime Sabartés, inviting him to come and share his apartment in Paris. Sabartés served as his secretary and lived with him, or nearby, for the next ten years.

Picasso painted very little at this time; he made a large number of engravings, mostly for Vollard, and began to write poetry which was published in the influential journal, *Cahiers d'Art.* He produced some portraits of Marie-Thérèse under the influence of his sullen mood, which he refused to show to anybody. He had re-introduced the bull into his canvases after a holiday to Spain in 1934, painting scenes of extreme cruelty and mutilation. A year later, his paintings and etchings sounded an even more pronounced note of violence and warning. The minotaur, a mythological half bull, half man, became a more prominent feature of his work, snorting furiously, symbolizing human bestiality and the destructiveness of the modern age. Picasso was soon to use this imagery to denounce the inhumanity of an event which affected him more deeply than anything he had ever before experienced. By July 1936, word had spread of the civil unrest in Spain and Picasso, like many other artists at the time, took a public stand and became passionately involved through his art in the plight of his native people, now suffering the brutal consequences of political dictatorship.

Marie-Thérèse (Musée Picasso, Paris) Cubist-style portrait of Marie-Thérèse Walter, who became Picasso's new mistress when his marriage to Olga began to sour. This portrait was painted in 1937, when this relationship had also cooled and Picasso had already moved on to his new mistress, Dora Maar.

CHAPTER 4

The War Years and Later Works

An atmosphere of discontent had been gathering strength in Spain for five years. The antiquated monarchy eventually collapsed, making room for a democratic government in 1931. It was christened the Second Republic and was dominated by professionals and the middle-classes.

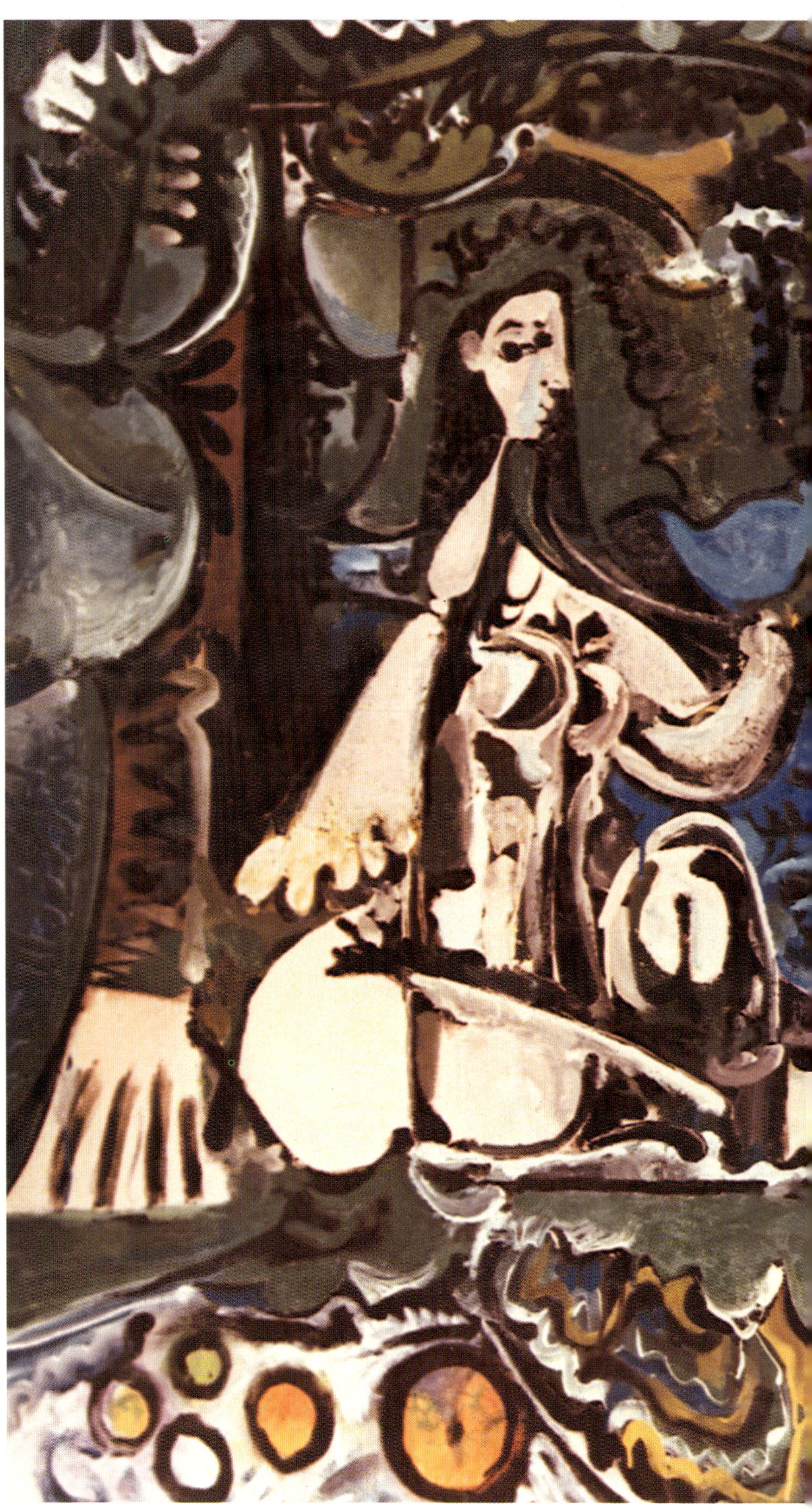

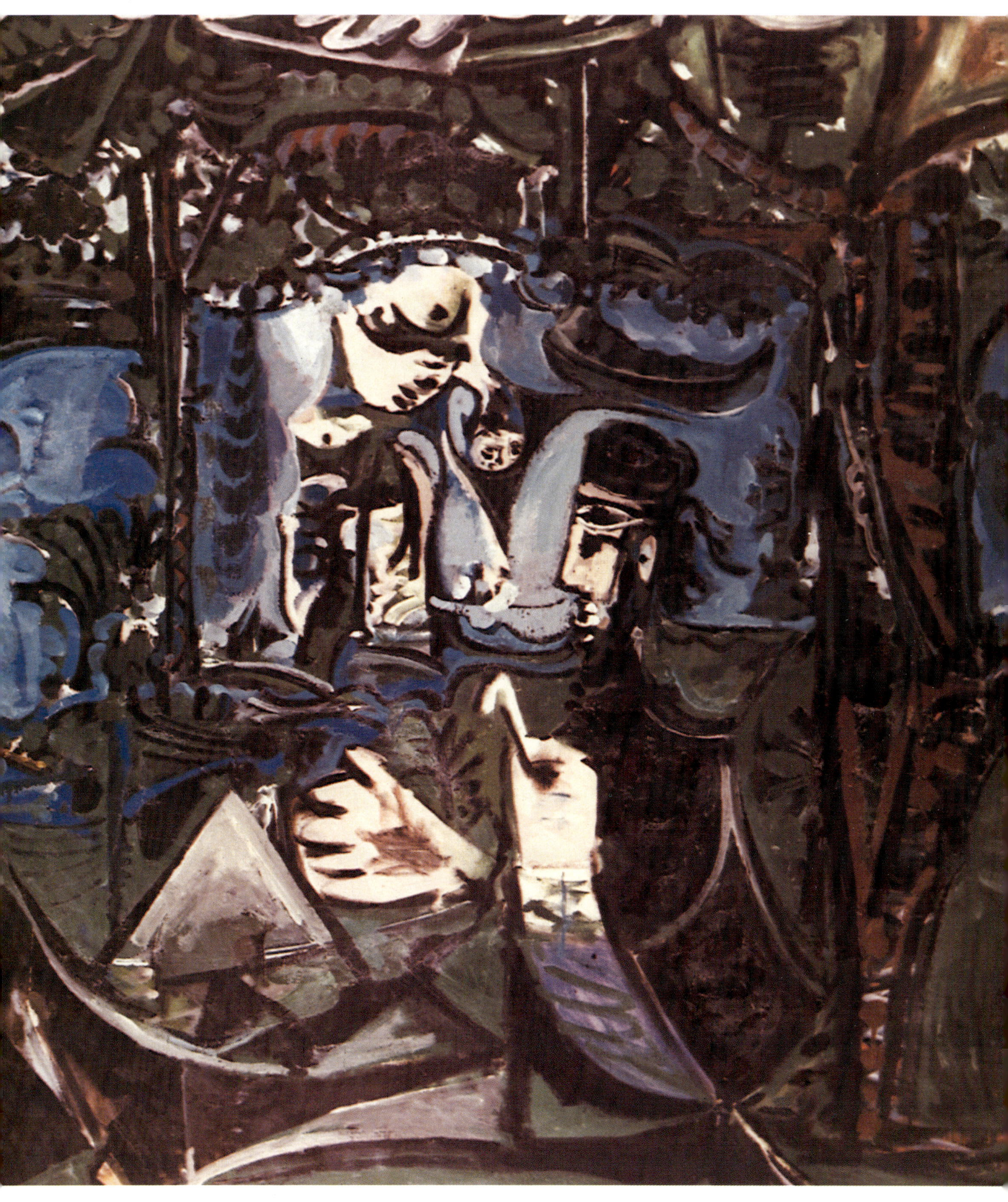

Overleaf:
Picnic after Manet, 1961 (Musée Picasso, Paris) Picasso enjoyed painting variations of his favourite classical paintings. Manet completed his *Déjeuner sur l'Herbe* in 1863 and it scandalized the art world. Picasso's canvas contains all the basic elements of Manet's work. The 'painter and model' theme was to occupy him now until his death in 1973.

Opposite:
Portrait of Dora Maar, 1937 (Musée Picasso, Paris) Picasso met Dora while on a trip to the South of France in 1936. She had lived in Argentina as a child and could converse with him easily in Spanish. A photographer by profession, Dora was responsible for the remarkable series of photographs featuring Picasso at work on *Guernica.*

Spain's new leaders had great difficulty holding on to the reigns of power, since the country was essentially feudal and the overwhelming demands for change could not be met at a satisfactory pace. From the outset, the Republic was weak and divided into factions. Many of its members had their own interests at heart and failed to introduce crucial industrial and agrarian reforms. The shortfall paved the way for a new party, the Popular Front, which came to power in February 1936. This substitute government also included a good many Republicans who had now joined ranks with Communists and Socialists. Some reforms were introduced, but the new regime still failed to placate the masses who continued to demand more improvements. By July, Spain's cities were at a standstill, striking workers could no longer tolerate their appalling conditions; the strikes erupted into riots and the upheaval spread rapidly.

Generalissimo Francisco Franco was forty-three years old when he pronounced himself Spain's Head of State. He had made full use of the climate of social unrest, seizing the opportunity to place his Rebel Army in a strategic position of so-called 'aid' to those opposing the National Front government. Within a few months, civil war between Republicans and Fascists raged in Spain. By October, Franco controlled almost half of the country and had installed a military dictatorship. Nazi Germany supplied him with bombs and weapons, while the Soviet Union furnished the Republicans with large quantities of arms and instructed its workers to donate a small portion of their monthly wage to the Spanish Republican cause.

After thirty years in exile, Picasso still remained very attached to his native Spain. He was deeply disturbed by the brutal military confrontation between Republicans and Fascists and, from the beginning, his political loyalty never wavered. No war had ever before attracted the interest of writers and artists on such a global scale, and they responded passionately to the threat of Franco's totalitarianism. Picasso embarked on a tireless campaign in support of the Republic's struggle for its life. He sold many of his paintings and donated the large sums of money to the Republican cause. He accepted the Republic's invitation to become Director of the Prado Museum and began organizing the evacuation of Spain's great art treasures, anticipating correctly that Franco's planes would eventually attempt to destroy the Museum. His anger intensified when the Prado was bombed and his personal hatred for the Fascist dictator was unleashed in a series of etchings entitled *The Dream and Lie of Franco.* There were eighteen engravings in this collection, which Picasso completed within two days in January, 1937. He intended to sell the etchings separately to add to the Republican defence fund, but they were eventually sold all together, complete with a hand-written poem composed by the artist. The drawings feature distressingly violent images of helpless

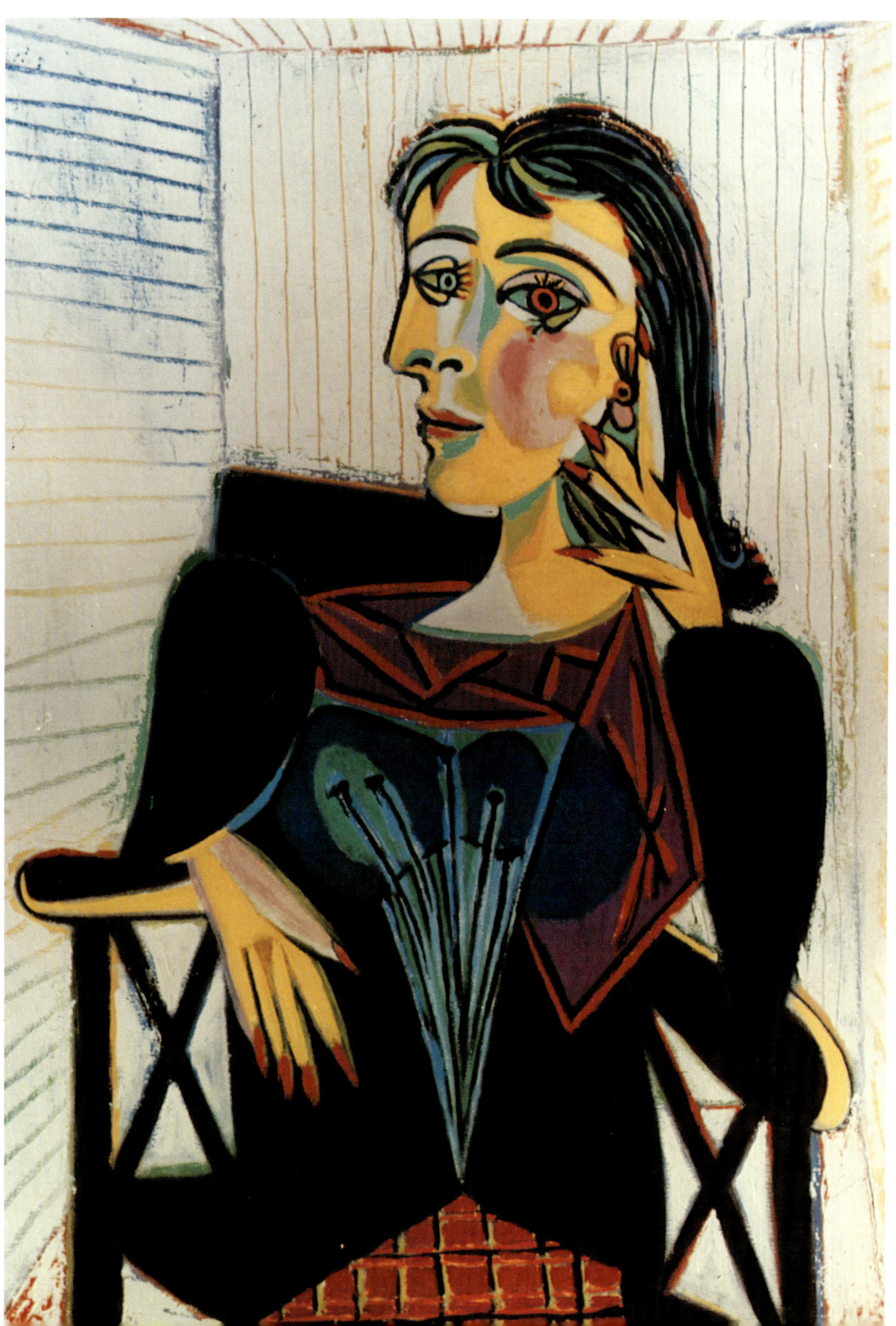

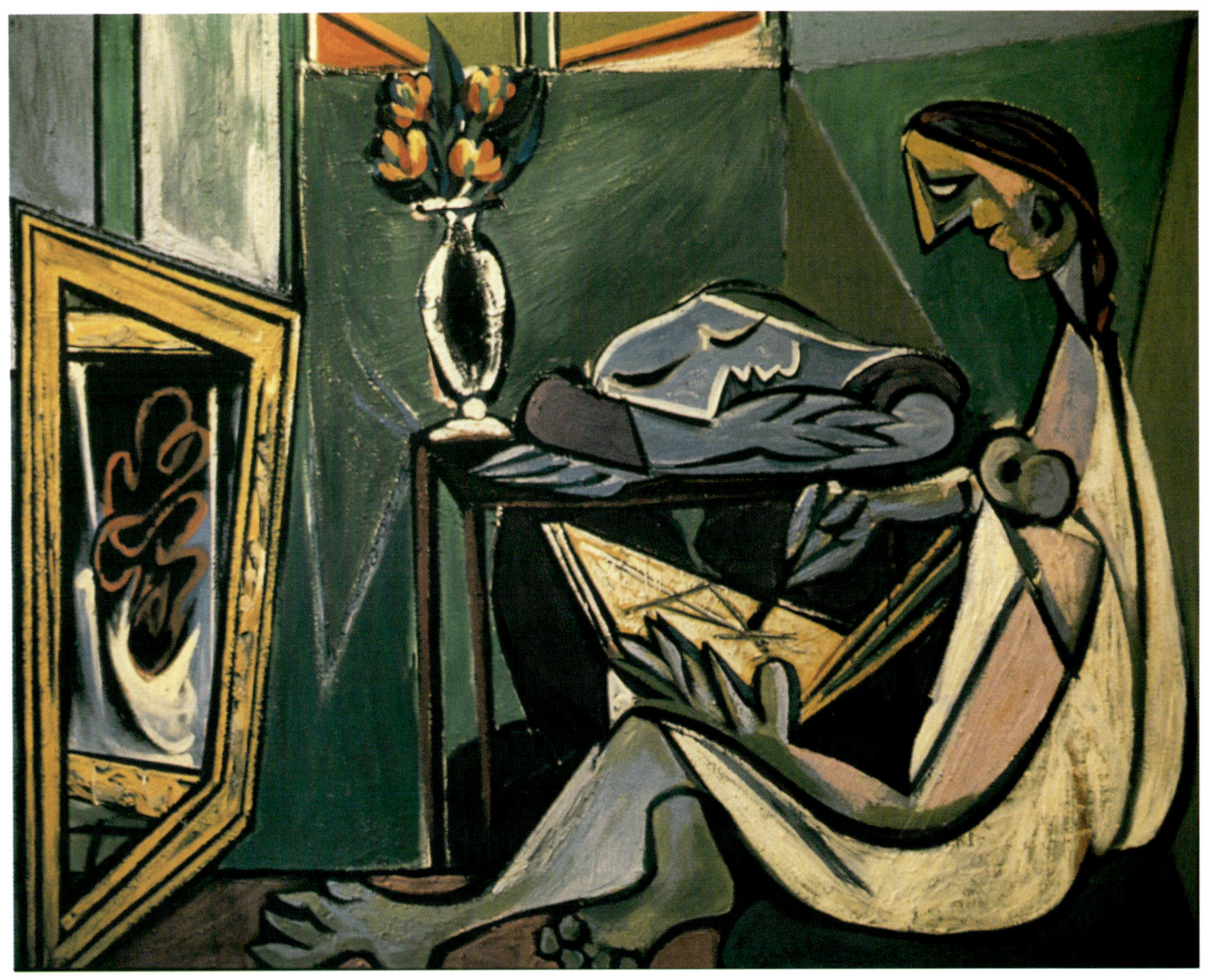

***Interior with a Young Girl*, 1935 (Musée National d'Art Moderne, Paris)**
Another portrait of Marie-Thérèse Walter, with a variation of the frontal view of the face containing a profile, which was typical of his Cubist paintings. Here, however, Picasso has abandoned the round face in favour of a full profile view.

women and children who lie slaughtered or dying. Franco is depicted as a louse with a large snout and coarse, bristle-like hair. In one of the drawings he attacks a classical monument with a pickaxe; in another he walks on a tightrope holding a Catholic banner attached to an enormous penis. In a third drawing, he kneels before a shrine surrounded by barbed wire and worships the money before him. Picasso's poem serves to complement the visual images which demonstrate his loathing of Franco:

> *... fandango of shivering owls souse of swords of evil-omened polyps scouring brush of hairs from priests' tonsures standing naked in the middle of the frying-pan placed upon the ice-cream cone of cod fish fried in the scabs of his lead-ox heart ...*

The Dream and Lie of Franco had not yet been published before a second request had been made for propagandist material. The

Republican government entreated Picasso to deliver an even larger artistic commentary on the war – a mural which would adorn the Spanish Republic's pavilion at the Paris World Fair in the summer of 1937. Picasso enthusiastically accepted the commission and rented two floors of a large seventeenth-century mansion near the banks of the river Seine. He had no firm idea what to paint. In the months leading up to April, he completed several pictures which reflect a deep unrest and an inner perplexity. *Bathers with a Toy Boat,* completed in February 1937, has none of the gay, warm atmosphere of his 1922 painting, *Women Running on a Beach,* painted on a similar theme. Picasso's holidaymakers are now scarcely recognizable as such. They resemble hard, angular wood-carvings, with monstrous heads, pointed breasts, distended stomachs and huge protruding buttocks. Picasso also produced several portraits of Marie-Thérèse at this time, who remained in the background of his life, and he painted his new mistress, Dora Maar, a Yugoslavian photographer whom he had met while on holiday in St Tropez the previous summer.

The series of etchings which paved the way for *Guernica,* the twentieth century's most terrifying document of the horrors of war, was produced in the early thirties for Ambroise Vollard as part of the *Vollard Suite.* These etchings depict the minotaur figure, originally borrowed from the Surrealists, yet amended to reflect a dual personality. The minotaur appears in a variety of settings where he encounters humankind. Sometimes the creature is mellow and gentle, at other times he is savage and lustful. He arouses sympathy when he is wounded or blinded, and stirs feelings of revulsion when he disembowels a horse. The drawings invite us to consider the extent to which the minotaur reflects mankind's behaviour, also unpredictable, and subject, at times, to the uncontrollable demands of an inner demon.

In 1935, Picasso continued this theme in a rather large etching entitled *Minotauromachie (War of the Minotaur).* In this mythical drawing, a young girl, who appears to represent innocence or frailty, fearlessly holds up a candle to the rapidly advancing minotaur, whose violent, threatening presence does not seem to discourage her. Between the two lies a horse, its entrails hanging loose, bearing the body of a dead female matador with exposed chest. On the left, a bearded man flees in terror from the bull-like creature, while the female couple, seated at the window where two doves rest, stare complacently at the scene below them. Picasso's precise intentions, conveyed through a mixture of Greek legend and modern fable, are difficult to fathom, but the allegorical figures of the mythical bull, the disembowelled horse and the dead matador were to feature in many works to follow. A sense of the ever-present dark side of human life which pervades this large engraving, was a theme Picasso returned to repeatedly in future works.

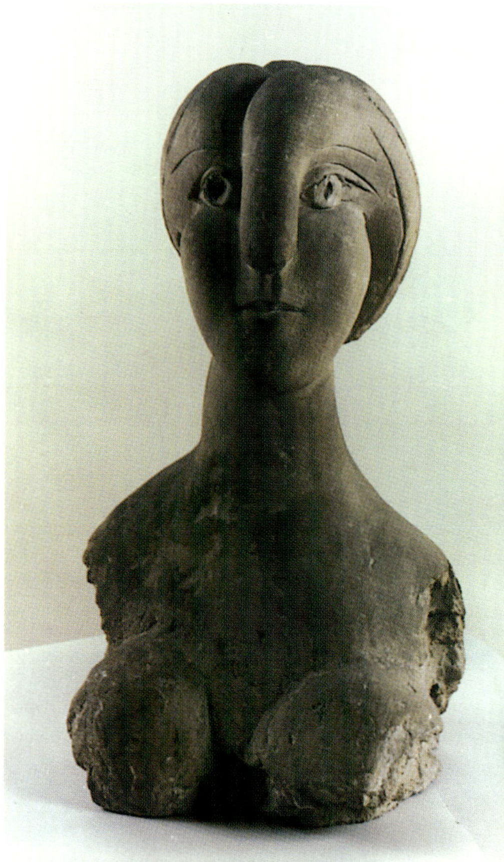

Woman's Bust, **1931 (Musée Picasso, Paris)** Picasso completed many of his sculptures of women's heads at his studio at Boisgeloup. They feature women with bulging, protruding noses. This bust, inspired by Marie-Thérèse Walter, refuses to pander to a feminine image of classical elegance.

Overleaf:
Maya with a Doll, **1938 (Musée Picasso, Paris)** The turbulent social atmosphere of the late thirties infiltrated even this portrait of Picasso's young daughter, Maya. The face, portrayed as a fusion of profile and frontal view, has a sinister expression, which completely overwhelms any impression of childlike innocence.

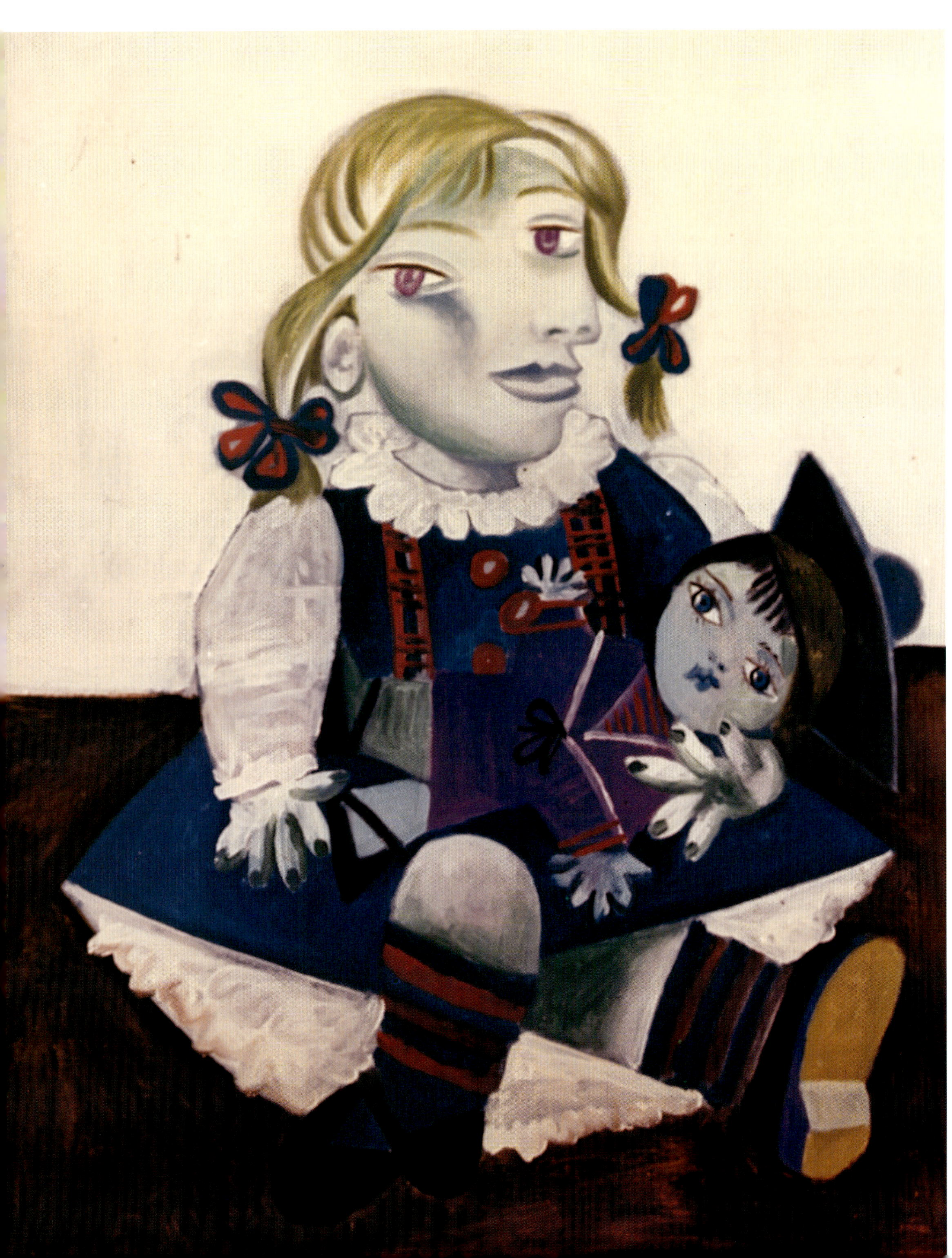

He was still procrastinating over the subject matter for his Republican mural when Franco's planes, displaying the German swastika, wiped out the small Basque town of Guernica on April 26, 1937. It was a market-day and the streets were crowded with shoppers. The bombing lasted for over three and a half hours; low-flying planes with machine-guns fired at the town's inhabitants who had taken refuge in the fields, and almost two thousand civilians lost their lives. Guernica had no strategic value whatsoever for Franco; the bombardment was simply a military exercise to test the effectiveness of explosive and incendiary bombs on a civilian population. The world had never before experienced the mass murder of innocents by such means, and for such mercenary purposes. The event had a devastating impact on Picasso and he was immediately spurred into action.

Between the first of May and the end of June 1937, he made about forty-five sketches for *Guernica.* Drawings completed on even the first day, contain the vital elements of the final painting and highlight its path of evolution. Within ten days, twenty-five sketches were made containing the bull to the left, the wounded horse in the centre of the picture and the light-bearer with outstretched arm above the horse. The studio in which Picasso worked was only just long enough to house the gigantic canvas. A series of photographs taken by Dora Maar, reveals how he was forced to work on the painting in a slanted position with the aid of a ladder. The canvas measured approximately twenty-five feet in width and twelve feet in height.

Picasso was not interested in depicting the destruction of Guernica with any great historical accuracy; he was not inspired to reflect military conflict in his art like a photographer. He set out instead to create a work of provocative symbolism, where the suffering of war could be interpreted in the context of a timeless evil for which all mankind was responsible. Apart from the title of the painting, *Guernica* does not conform to a fixed principle of space and time. It is not an eye-witness account, nor is it an allegorical piece. It is a tidal wave of emotion, crashing forth from the depths of an utterly tormented soul on to the artist's canvas.

The violence and futility of war are conveyed through figures free of conventional appearances; the painting is a fusion of styles Picasso had practised over the years. The flat perspective of figures with disembodied limbs and dislocated eyes and ears mirrors his Cubist paintings and his preoccupation with primitive art. The minotaur of his previous etchings also features prominently. The colours are chosen for their dramatic and emotional effect and the painting displays a skilful manipulation of light and shade. The artist's palette is limited to the use of blacks and charcoal greys, offset by an unwelcome, bleaching white, serving to illuminate the physical pain and the contorted, shrieking forms of the afflicted.

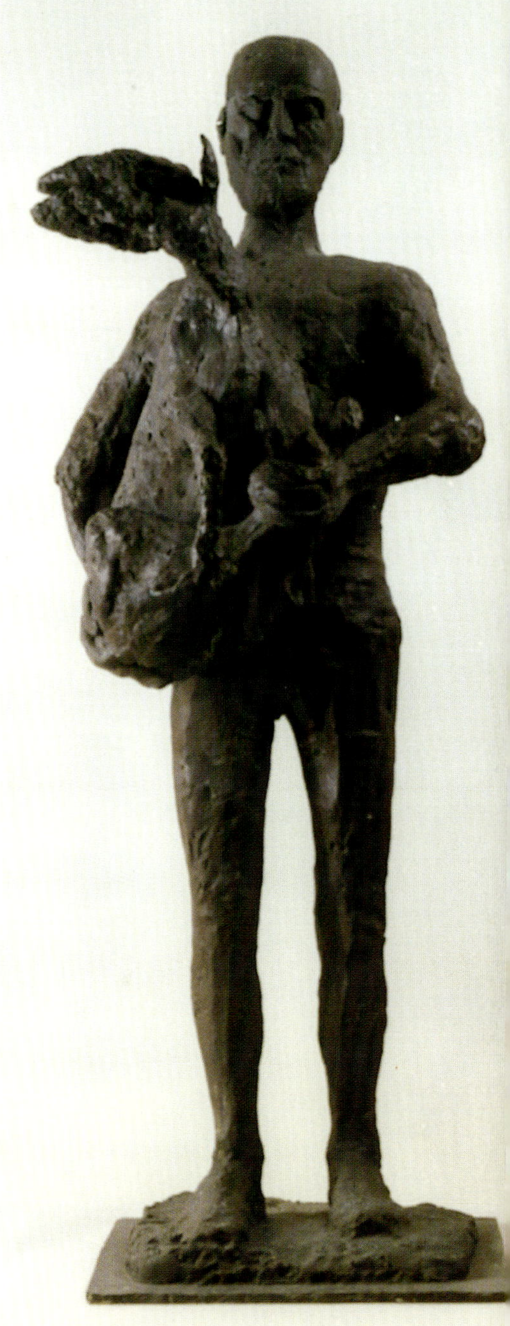

Shepherd with Sheep, **1943 (Paris, Musée Picasso)** Picasso completed this sculpture in the summer of 1943. Materials were extremely difficult to come by and the clay was stolen for him by a Spanish friend. The calming, pastoral theme of the piece was in deliberate contrast to the nightmare of the Second World War. The sculpture remains one of Picasso's most valuable pieces.

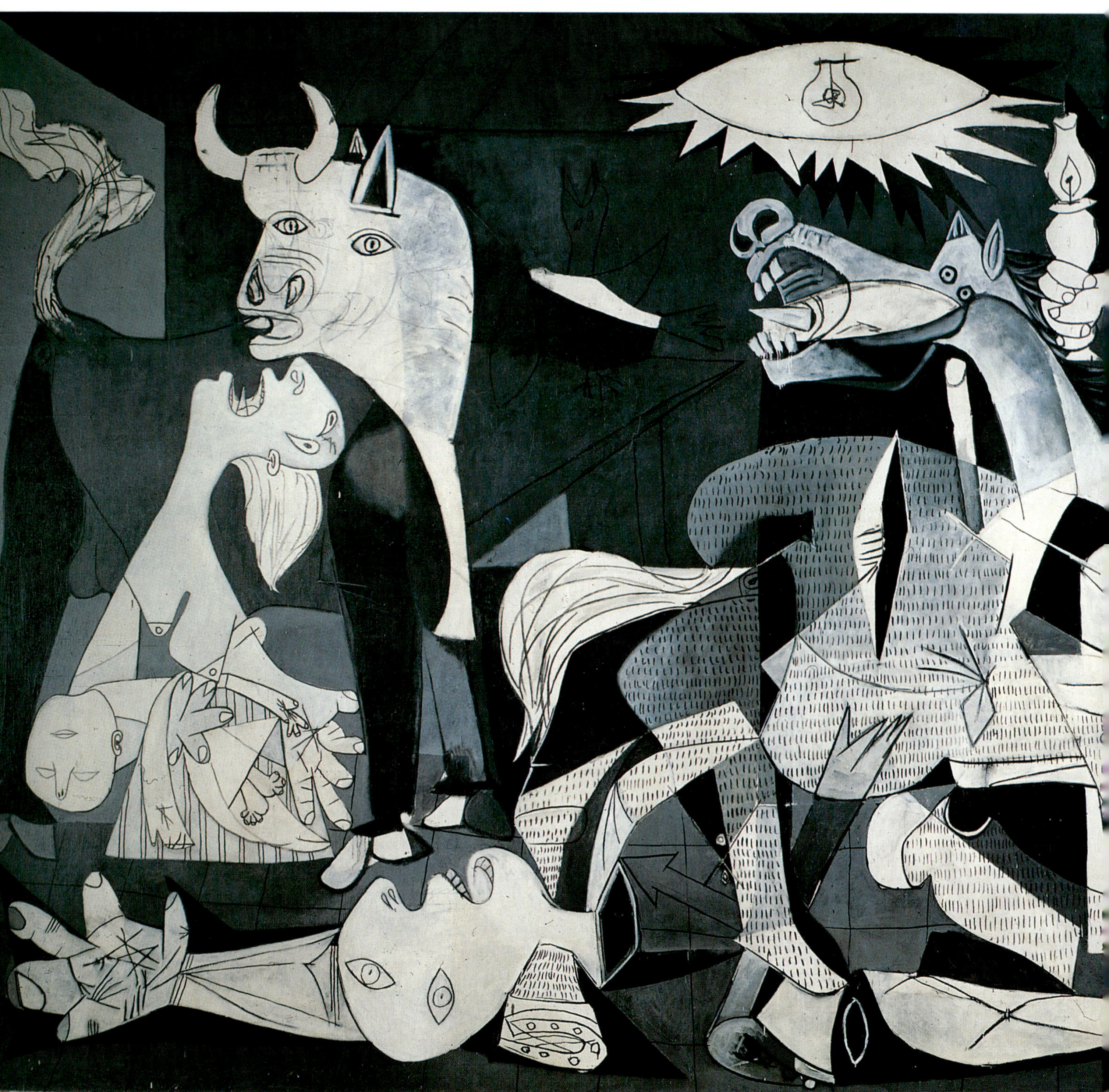

'The horse represents the people,' Picasso revealed in an interview to an American airman in 1944, 'the bull is not Fascism, but it is brutality and darkness.' He built up the painting detail by detail, displaying a remarkable stamina for a man of fifty-six years. The neighing, wounded horse occupying the centre of the picture conveys a horror never previously achieved on a canvas. The animal is entirely defence-

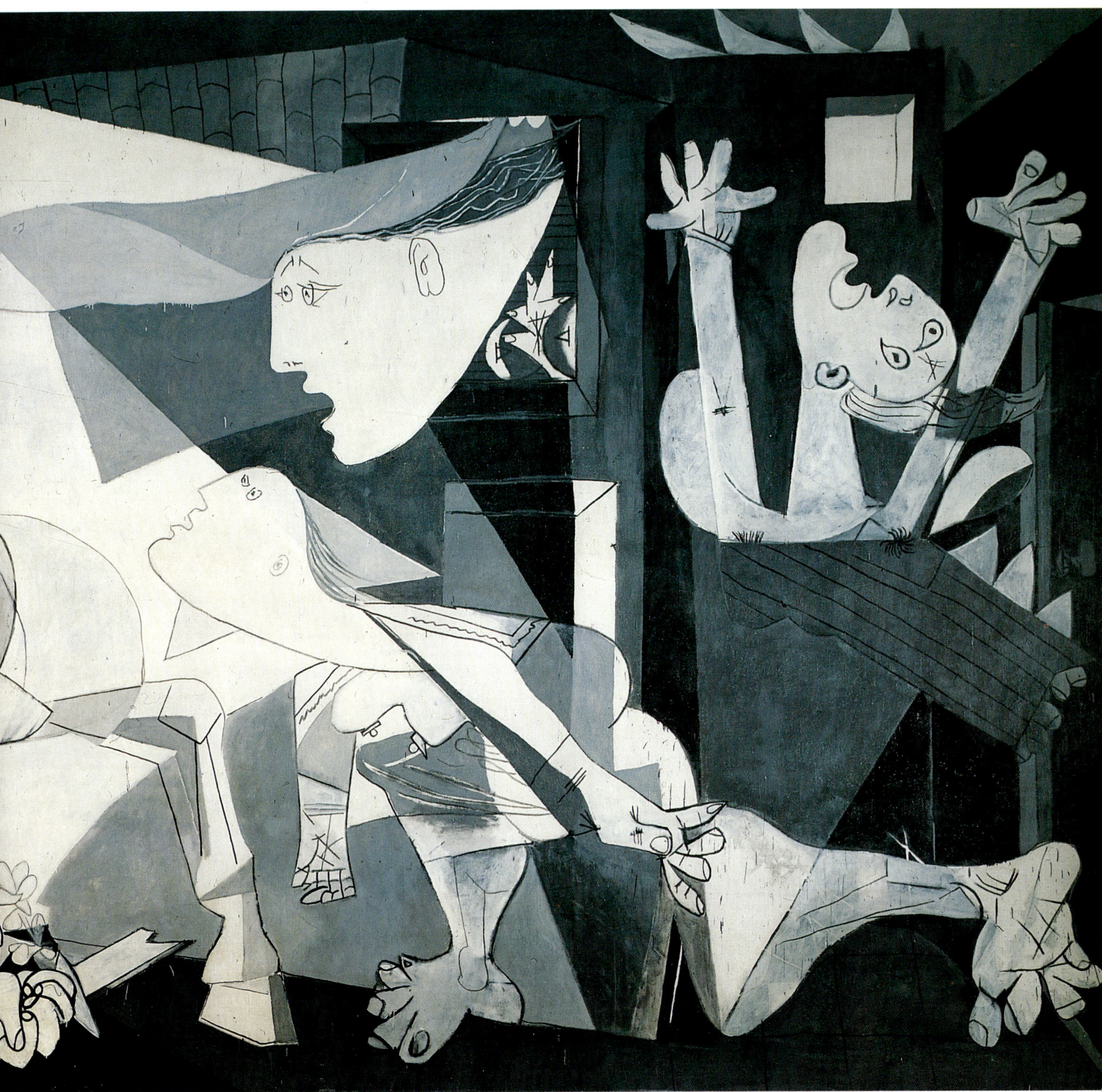

less, consumed by fear, its terror made almost audible through its gaping mouth. The dying figures around the horse mimic the terrified, twisted expression. The figure on the right, with its hands thrown into the air and its wide-open mouth, imitates the posture of a bellowing, sacrificial animal. The dismembered head of a warrior towards the left of the picture reveals a similarly horrific facial expression, while the mother clutching her child's dead body has arched her head back in an abandon of grief, flinging her mouth open to reveal a sharp, spike-shaped tongue. The bull, with flared nostrils and erect tail, stands menacingly over her, bodies are trampled underfoot, the lamp-bearer sheds light on the scene of destruction, and the ferocious creature seems about to charge and add further to the carnage all around it.

Guernica was finished after two months of exhausting work. It was then installed in the Spanish pavilion in Paris where it met with a storm of controversy. Franco's supporters were incensed by Picasso's work. Art critics were divided in their opinion of the canvas. One review denounced its 'scarecrow figures', another criticized its 'banality of overstatement', a third praised the painting's 'intensest passion' which made it a 'great work of art, transcending all schools and categories'. *Guernica* gained worldwide recognition at the International

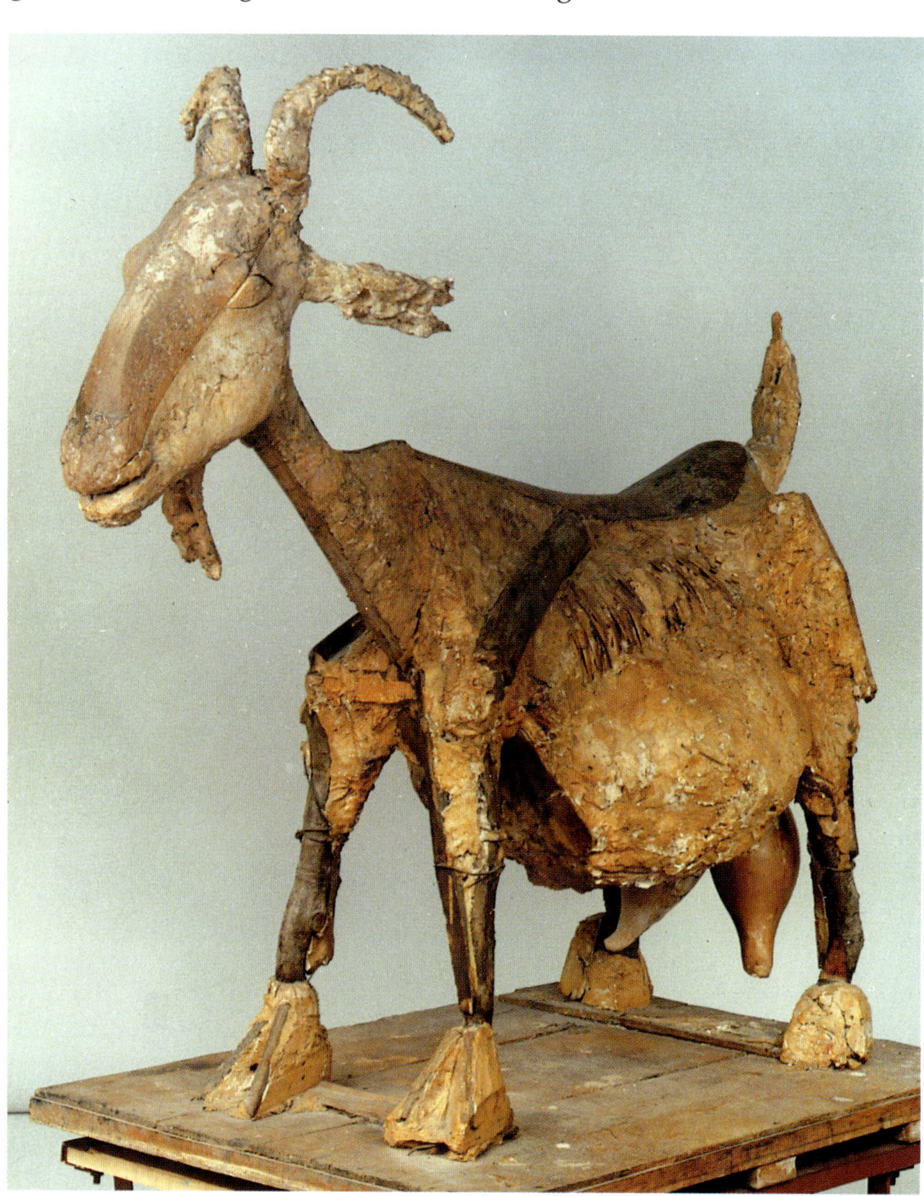

***The Goat*, 1950 (Musée Picasso, Paris)** Picasso's goat, created in his studio at Vallauris, is a highly skilful moulding together of everyday objects to form an astoundingly accurate animal image. His materials include a wicker basket, flower pots, fragments of china, palm leaves and odd pieces of metal tubing.

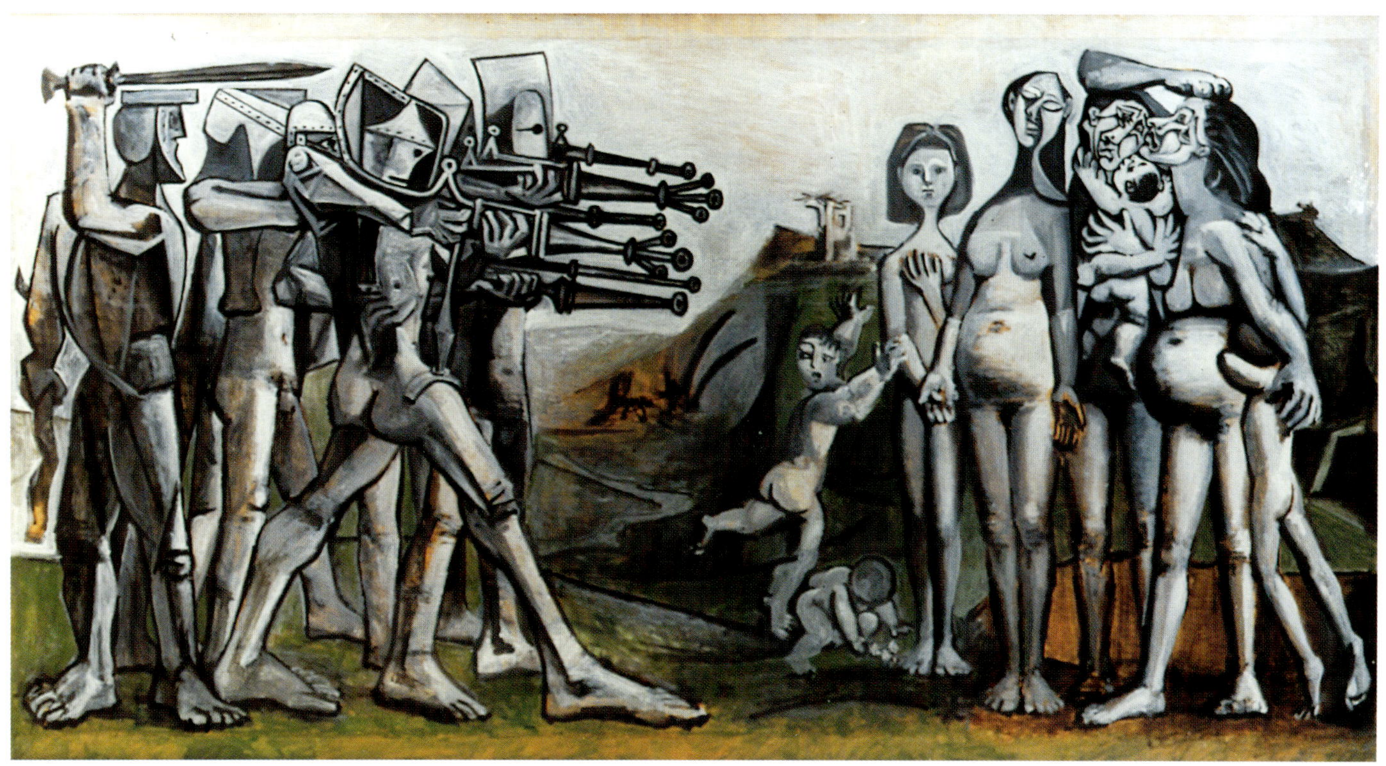

Exhibition and it rapidly became a symbol of Spain's tragic armed struggle for identity. Picasso decreed that the painting should not be housed in his native country until Fascism had been eradicated and a democratic government restored to power. In 1981, after more than forty years of exile in New York, the picture was returned to Spain where it is now proudly exhibited at the Prado Museum in Madrid.

The years which followed Picasso's painting of *Guernica* were dominated by similar artistic themes and concerns. After the Second World War Picasso remarked: 'I did not paint the war ... But there is no doubt that the war is there in the pictures which I painted then.' *Guernica* and *Charnel House* explicitly reflect the tyranny of Fascism, but *Weeping Woman*, a portrait of Dora, painted in the autumn of 1937, presents an equally powerful and disturbing image of human suffering. The expression of grief, bordering on rage, is stifled by a handkerchief crammed into the woman's mouth. It cannot stem the flow of her huge tears which stream from dislocated eyes, presented simultaneously on the profiled face. Bright, garish colours, quite unlike the sombre tones of *Guernica,* clash angrily with each other and reinforce the impression of pain and frenzy. There is a similarly disturbed atmosphere in the painting of his daughter Maya with her doll, completed in 1938, where the child's innocent face is given a sinister, sneering expression. The picture entitled *Cat Devouring a Bird*, painted in 1939, is also a remarkably gruesome piece, offering a vivid image of nature's cruelty. One exceptional picture from this period, however, attempts to redress the artist's preoccupation with the theme of suffering. *Night Fishing in Antibes,*

Massacre in Korea, 1951 (Musée Picasso, Paris) Over the years, Picasso came to acknowledge painting as 'an instrument of war' to be waged against 'brutality and darkness'. He produced several paintings on this theme, with increasingly gruesome images, including those of innocent women and children, either lying slaughtered or about to face death.

painted while on holiday with Dora in August 1939, is a relaxed, harmonious painting of a fishing village, idyllically captured at full moon. Yet for all its cheerfulness, it exudes a consciousness that time is merely suspended, awaiting the imminent impact of reality.

By September 1939, the Nazis had invaded Poland. Picasso journeyed to Royan, a small Atlantic town north of Bordeaux, and spent almost a year there, declining to leave France even though he had been offered asylum by both the American and Mexican governments. He returned to Paris in 1940, now occupied by the Germans, and remained there for the duration of the war. Hitler had denounced his work as degenerate 'Bolshevik art' and he was not allowed to exhibit. Picasso refused to flirt with the Nazis; their lack of appreciation did not deter him in any way and the war years were some of his most prolific. He painted, sketched and sculpted furiously as if to distract his thoughts. 'This was not the moment for a creative man to throw in the sponge, accept defeat and stop work,' he later insisted. 'There was nothing to do but go on working seriously and enthusiastically struggle to find food, calmly continue to see one's friends, and await freedom.'

Many of the still-lifes produced during the war reflect the poverty and hunger of his circumstances. *Still Life with Steer's Skull*, with its morbid ox-skull as the central object, reflects the intolerably barren atmosphere of Paris, the dearth of food and warmth, the ever-present darkness of his surroundings. The sculpture *Death's Head*, produced in 1944, powerfully evokes a kindred atmosphere of decay. Picasso was forced to make use of whatever materials came to hand. Like most of the sculptures he produced at this time, *Death's Head* was modelled in plaster, as bronze was simply not available, and only cast in metal after the war.

The occupation of Paris ended in August 1944 and Picasso emerged as a symbol of courage and tenacity, becoming one of the most popular figures of liberated France. The committee of the Autumn Salon paid him an official tribute by offering him a whole gallery at a forthcoming exhibition, an honour previously bestowed on French artists only. He gratefully acknowledged this mark of respect and exhibited seventy-four paintings and five sculptures at the event. At the same time, he began work on *Charnel House*, one of the greatest canvases he painted after *Guernica*, inspired by the shocking news of the German concentration camps and, on a personal level, by the death of his life-long friend, Max Jacob, in one of the camps at Drancy. *Charnel House* is also painted in shades of black, grey and white, but the symbolism of *Guernica* is abandoned in favour of a more forthright representation of slaughter and dire starvation.

Charnel House effectively ended Picasso's exploration of macabre subjects which had preoccupied him during the war. He had joined the Communist party within a month of Paris' liberation and was more

Woman in an Armchair, **1960 (New Orleans Museum of Art)** Women were undoubtedly Picasso's single most important source of inspiration during his artistic career. Those who shared his life were a prominent feature of his painting, and he portrayed them in a wide variety of styles.

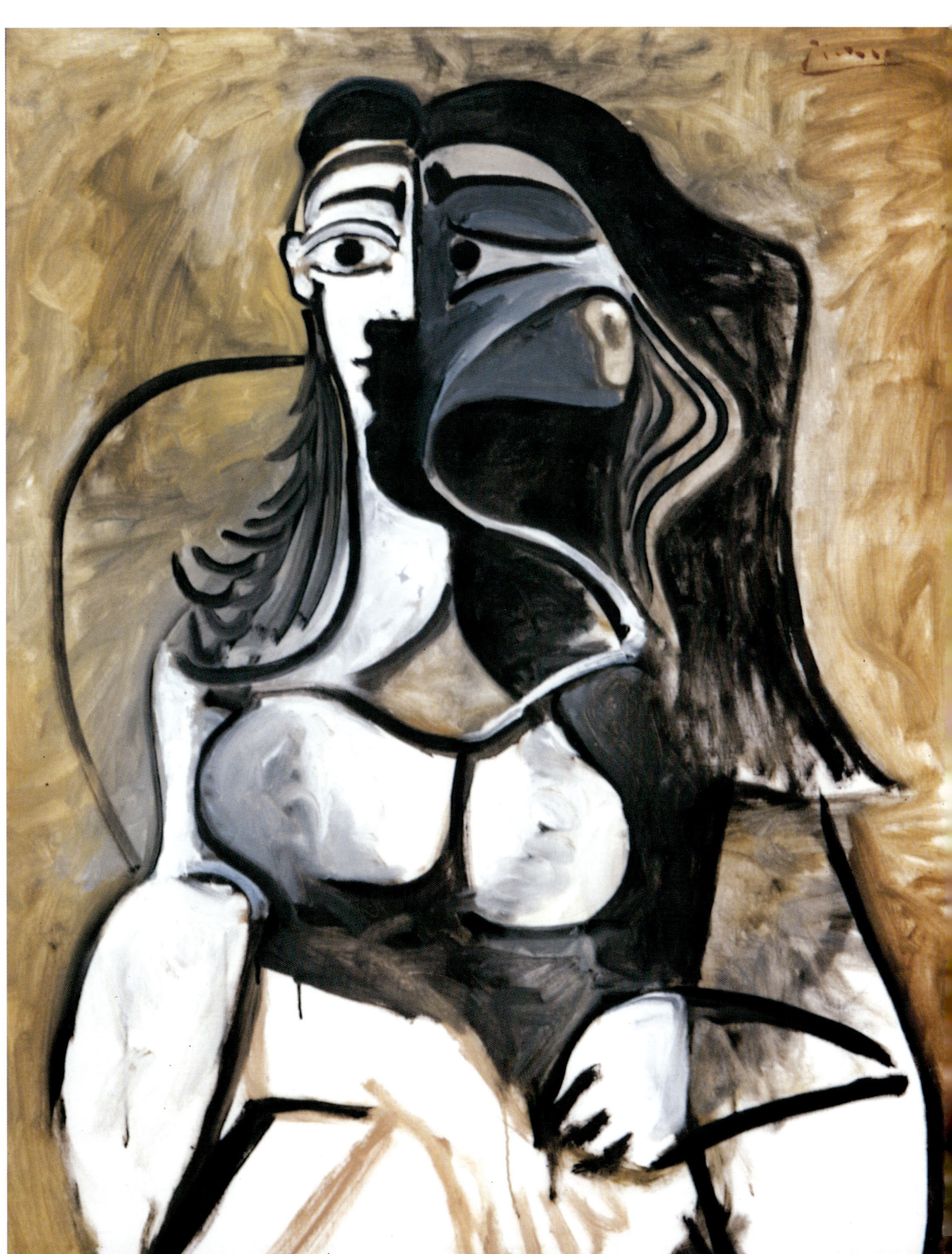

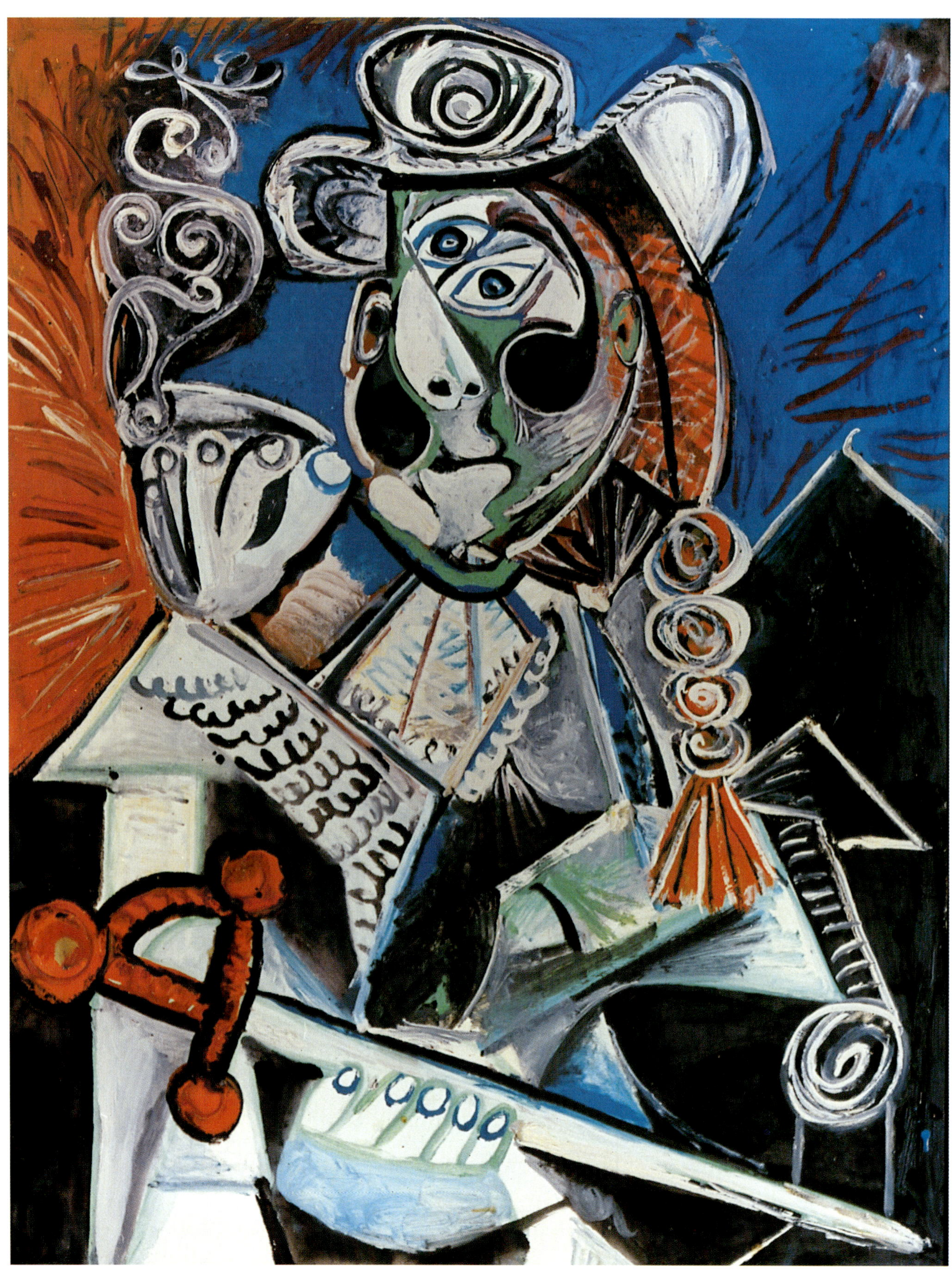

hopeful for the future as a result. New themes began to appear in his canvases and his creative energy spread to every available medium – to painting, sculpture, engraving, lithography and ceramics, which he now took up seriously for the first time. A series of lithographs produced in the autumn of 1945 at the workshop of Fernand Mourlot, France's most expert lithographer, now featured a new woman, Françoise Gilot. Although Picasso was three times her age, the two had much in common. Françoise was intelligent and independent, a huge admirer of Picasso's work and a painter of some talent herself. Picasso described her as 'a growing plant' and many of the paintings he completed of Françoise at this time, including *Joie de Vivre*, depict her as a flower-like creature, with a stem-shaped body and a face framed with petals and leaves. In the summer of 1946, they travelled together to Antibes where Picasso was offered a floor of the village's dilapidated museum to use as a studio. He had many fond memories of Antibes and worked with great energy during this visit, producing over thirty canvases throughout the summer months. All of them were light in theme and Mediterranean in atmosphere, reflecting the pleasure of his stay and the special inspiration the southern landscape seemed to hold for him. It was at this point that he made the decision to settle in the south of France with his new mistress.

By 1948, Picasso had become a father for the third time. He was now sixty-seven years old and Françoise was already expecting another child by him. He stayed at the small town of Vallauris until October, where he freely indulged his newly discovered passion for pottery. He began to refer to it as 'sculpture without tears' and, as had so often been the case before, he dramatically transformed a craft about which he had previously known very little. He went to work daily at the 'Madoura' pottery studio owned by Suzanne and Georges Raimé and within a short space of time, created extraordinarily unique pieces in this medium. Between 1947 and 1948, Picasso produced about two thousand items of ceramic art. Some of these objects were ordinary household utensils, others were metamorphosed into spectacular works of art with depictions of bull-fights, or birds, especially doves and owls. His later ceramic experiments involved a pottery collage effect, where several parts of different vessels were joined together to form objects no longer retaining their utility, yet recalling his experimental canvases of an earlier period.

Up until the very last years, Picasso never ceased to expand the field of his activities, but the price demanded, in terms of personal happiness, was often a substantially high one. He continued to paint and sculpt while feverishly involved with his ceramics. He was also deeply committed to the French Communist Party and was overjoyed, when in 1949, his lithograph of a pigeon was used by the Party as an advertisement for its forthcoming World Congress. He produced a

The Matador, **1970 (Musée Picasso, Paris)** Picasso's very first painting, at the age of nine, was a portrait of a matador. He used the image again and again throughout his career; the dead matador, in particular, was employed as a symbol of the violence of the modern age.

large number of 'Maternities' at this time, in which he captured his two children on canvas, playing or resting with their mother. He finished several sculptures also, many on a maternal theme, including *Pregnant Woman* and *Woman with a Baby Carriage*. The latter is an amusing construction, reintroducing Picasso's former practice of assembling odd pieces of junk metal to achieve a remarkably lifelike effect. *The Goat* and the wooden sculpture, *Woman Reading*, were created now also. He lived and breathed his work, allowing very little else to intrude into his almost obsessive, creative world.

After seven years of living with a fiercely determined and often self-absorbed partner, Françoise Gilot decided to leave Picasso and to return to Paris with the children. Picasso was now over seventy years old and Françoise's departure left him feeling isolated and miserable. He remained at Vallauris and threw himself into his work, completing, alongside numerous other projects, a series of one hundred and eighty drawings united by a theme of the artist and his model. The series entitled *Picasso and the Human Comedy* was essentially a tribute to women, yet infiltrated by feelings of bitterness at the fact that the artist was growing old and becoming increasingly impotent.

He did not remain alone for long, however. Jacqueline Roque, a cousin of Madame Raimé, who ran the pottery studio at Vallauris, first met Picasso in the summer of 1952 in Cannes and it was here that they moved in 1955, to a large nineteenth-century stately home known as 'La Californie'. Jacqueline, like many of the women Picasso admired before her, soon became the subject of his art and he produced a great many compelling portraits of her, revealing her large dark eyes and high cheekbones. At 'La Californie' he began work on one of his last major works, a set of variations of *Las Meninas* (The Maids of Honour) the seventeenth-century masterpiece by fellow Spanish artist, Diego Velázquez. Picasso's forty-four variations, produced between 1956 and 1957, were at once a parody of Velázquez' painting and a more serious exploration of the ambiguities of the original painting. Art itself had become a constantly recurring subject of his work and variations on historically famous paintings provided a means to explore this. Manet's *Le Déjeuner sur l'herbe* was also revived by Picasso at this time. His 1961 version examines again the theme of artist and model, which now occupied him until his death. Two features in this painting were used by Picasso again and again: the model is naked and the painter is nearly always depicted with cigarette in hand.

Picasso's later works after this date have no great revolutionary impact. He remained aloof from new art movements and drew his inspiration largely from his personal life, painting in whatever manner satisfied him. It is estimated that he produced over fifty thousand works of astounding variety during his lifetime. In his very last phases, he chose himself as subject, opting for a simplified approach and

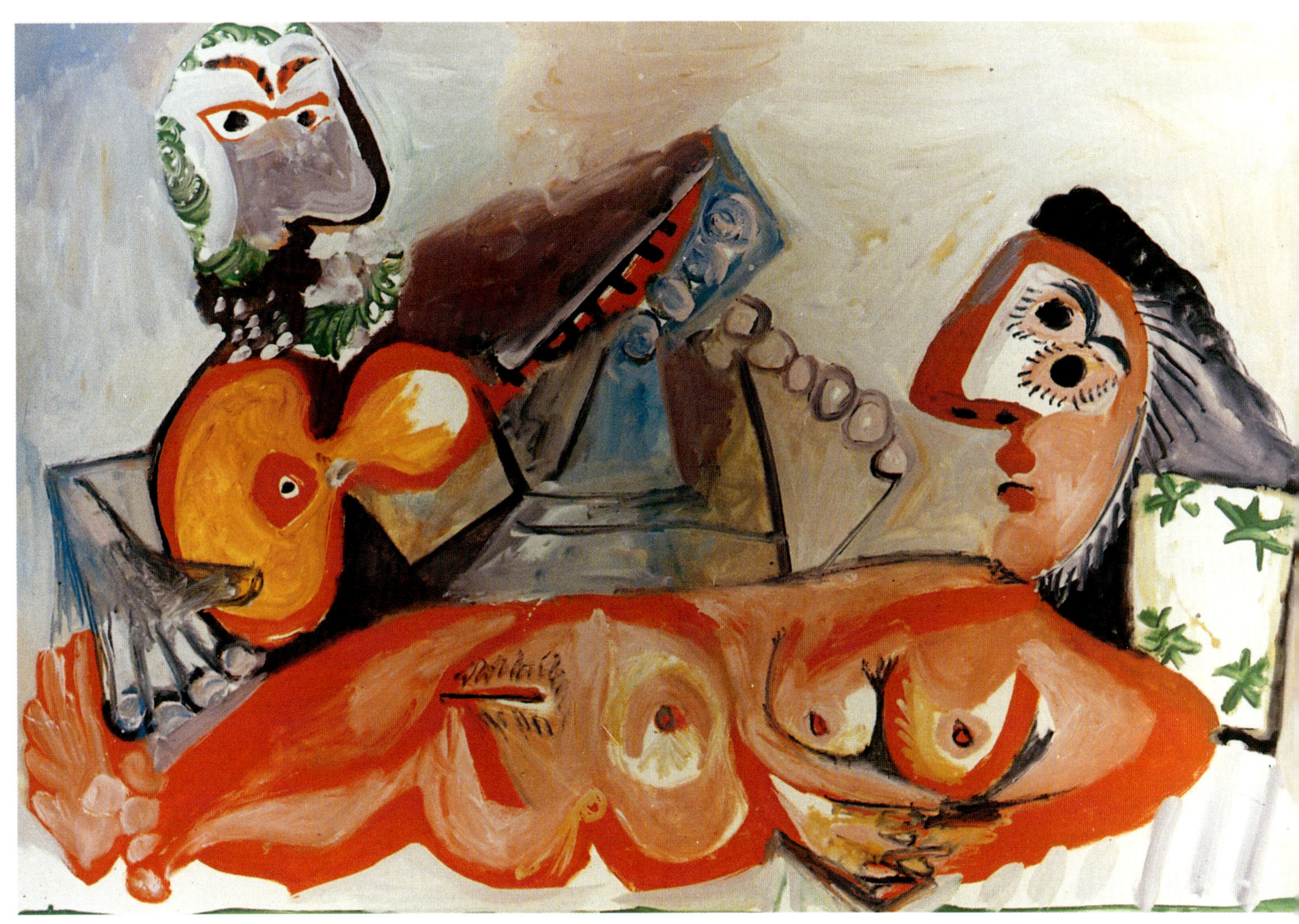

reducing the language of his art to an uncomplicated sketchiness, reminiscent, at times, of children's drawings. Picasso believed that 'completing something means killing it, depriving it of life and soul', his canvases became increasingly unadorned, almost as if he did not want to finish them and was willing himself to return to them at a later stage. He followed his intense personal commitment right to the very end, not once losing sight of the quest for a comprehensive understanding of his art. His extraordinary drive and incredible gifts are best summed-up in the words of the poet, and long-term friend of Picasso, Jaime Sabartés:

With him, there was never any hesitation: he came into the world with a painter's mission, and paint is what he would do, whatever the cost, without regard to anything else. By 'paint', I mean explaining himself through signs; expressing himself through plastic media; manifesting himself by communicating those things which had caught his attention, on which he had reflected with his brain: the manner of doing this counted for little.

Reclining Nude and Man Playing Guitar, 1970 (Musée Picasso, Paris)
Picasso believed that the painter 'never finishes', that he 'can never write "The End"'. Until his death in 1973, he was producing extraordinary work in a huge range of styles, always amazing his critics, or delighting his multitude of admirers.

INDEX

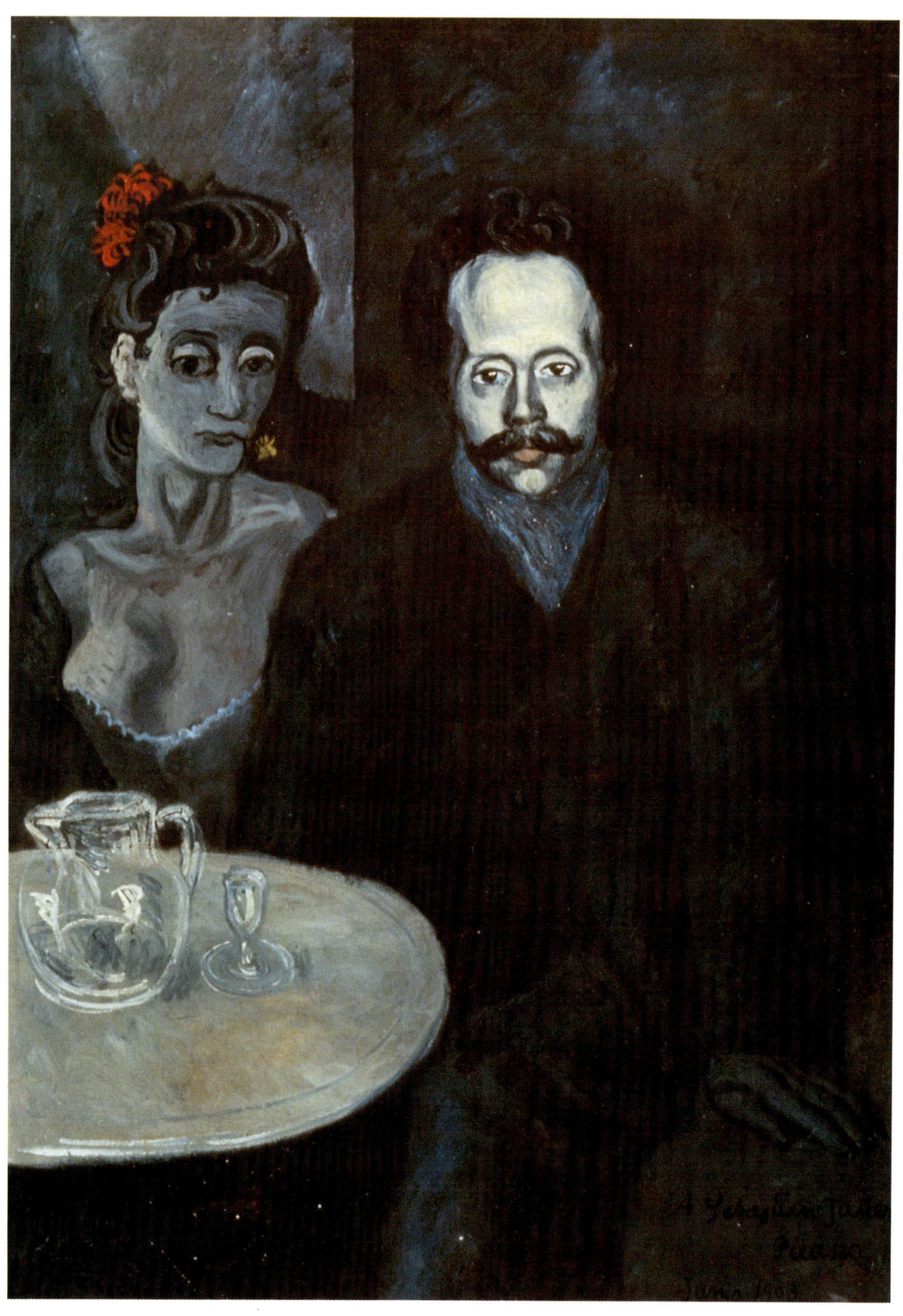

Picasso. *Portrait of Sebastian Junyer-Vidal*, 1903
(Los Angeles County Museum)

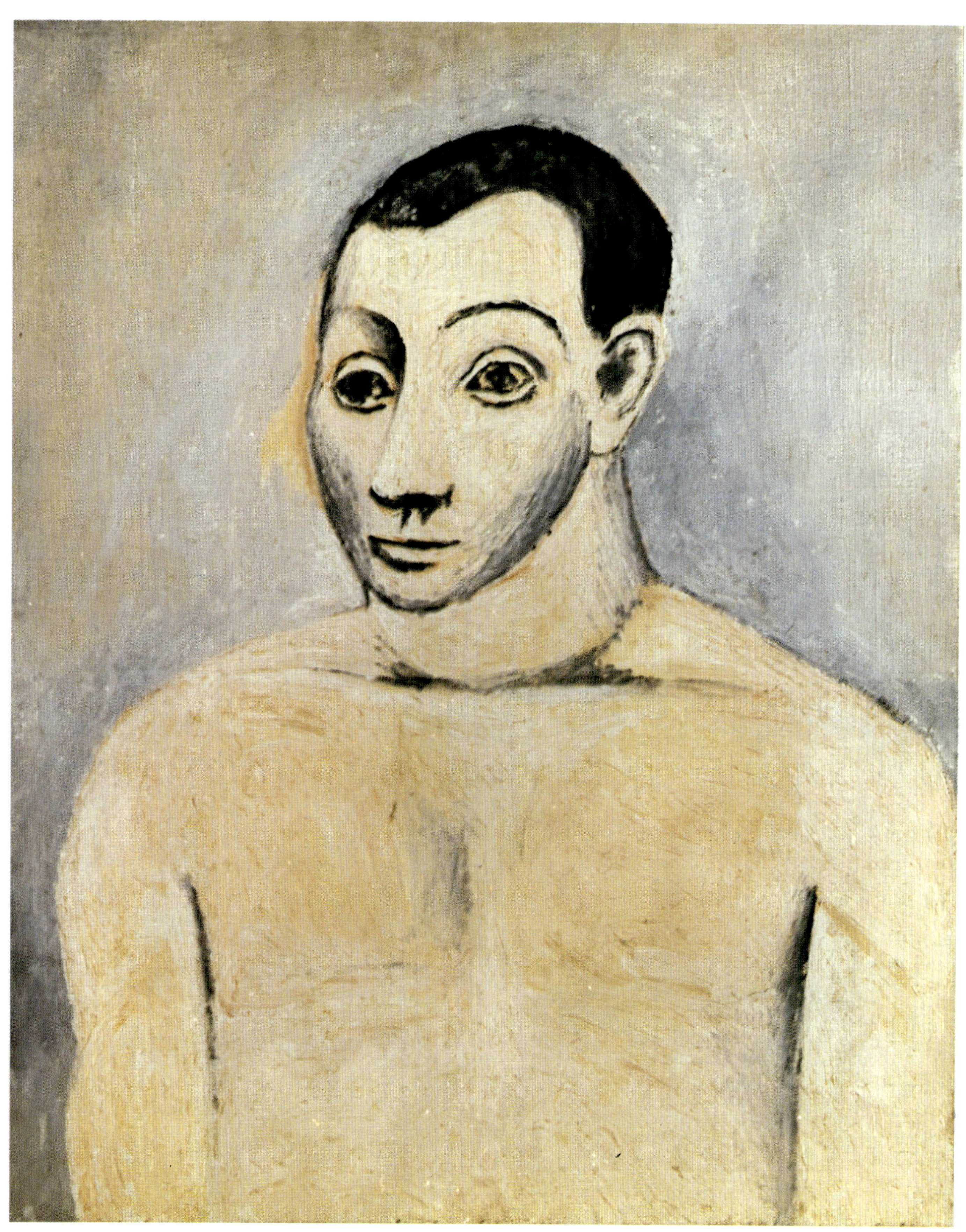

Picasso. *Self-Portrait,* **1906**
(Musée Picasso, Paris)

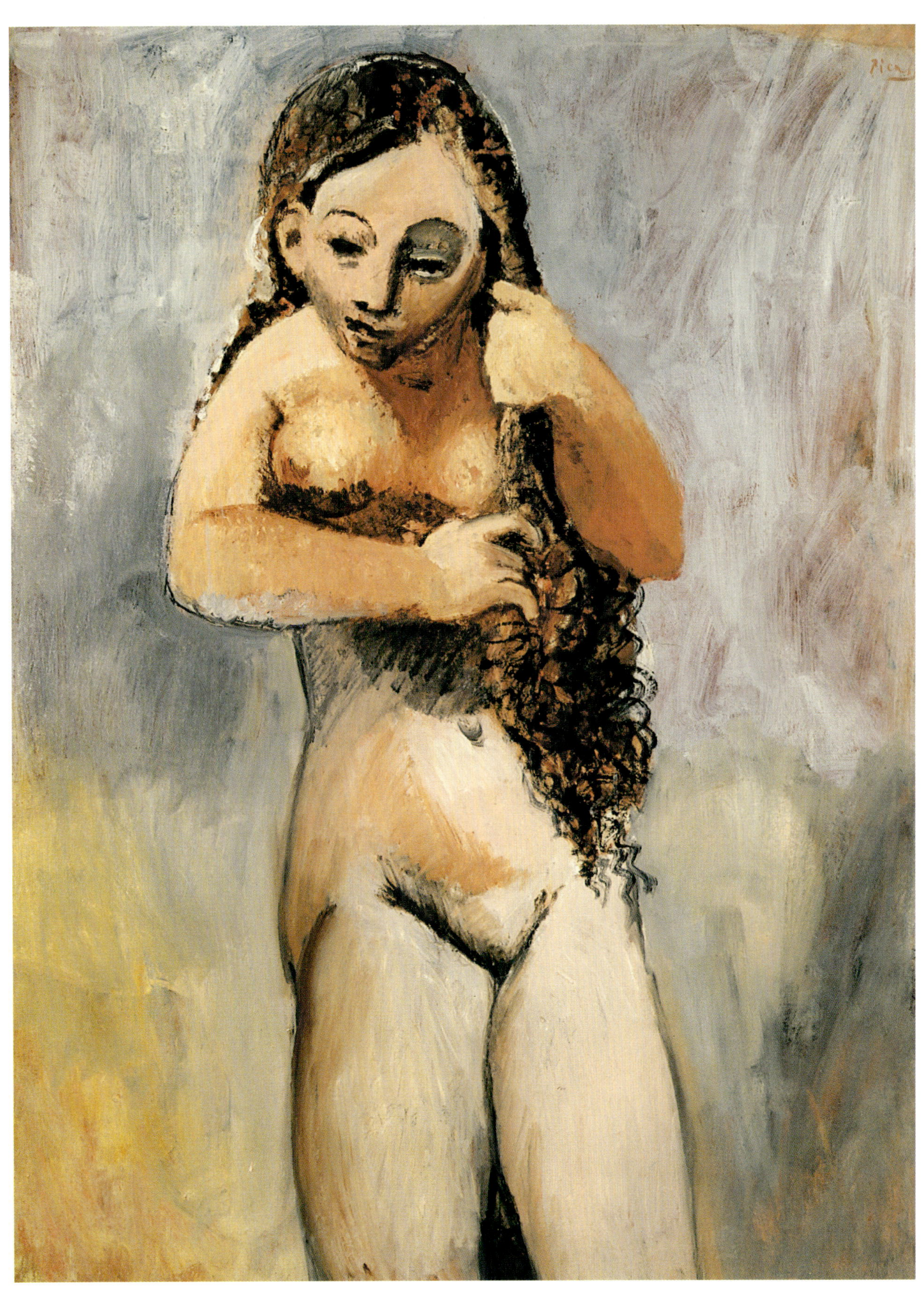

Picasso. *Woman Combing her Hair*
(Kimbell Art Museum, Fort Worth)

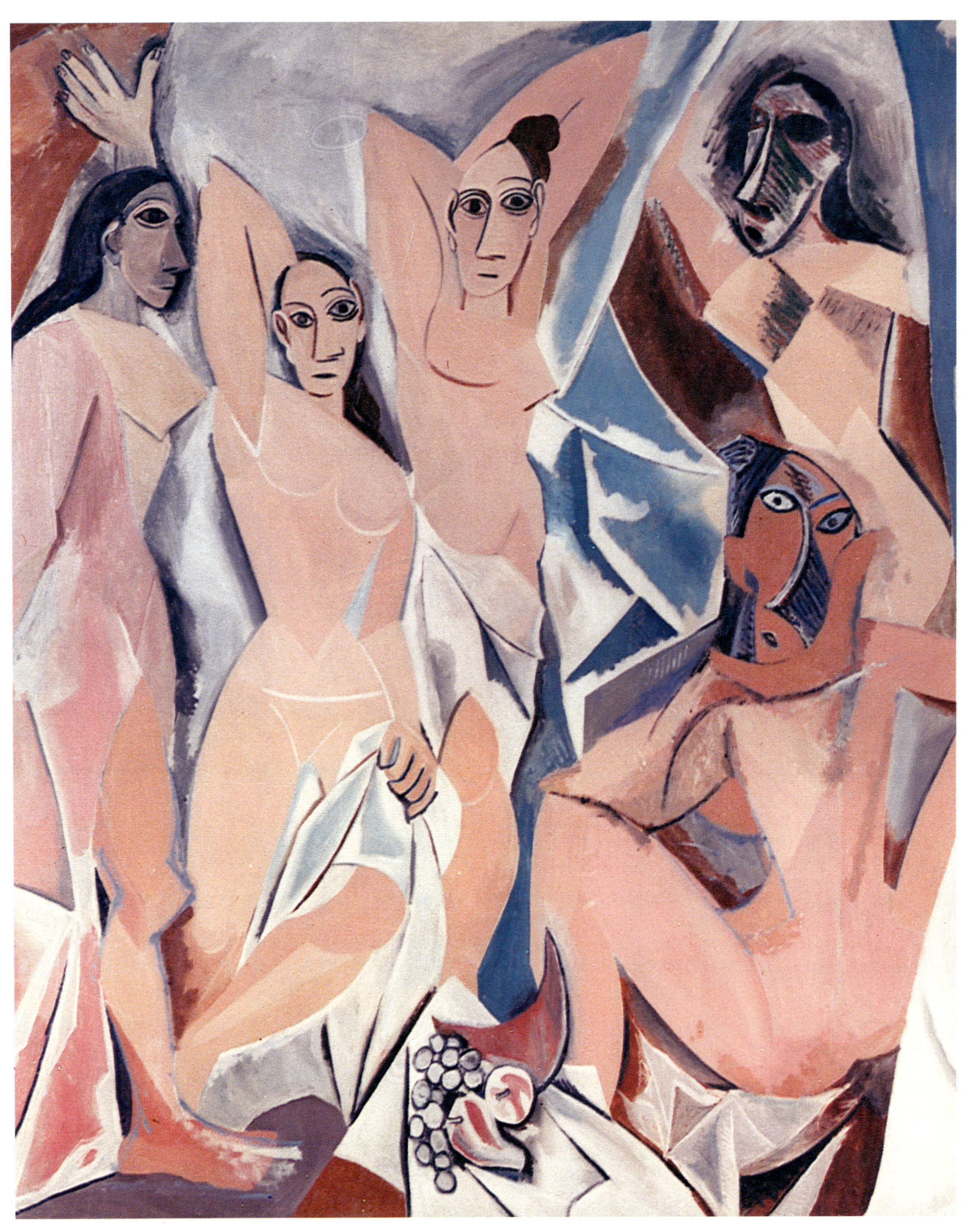

Picasso. *Les Desmoiselles d'Avignon,* **1907**
(Museum of Modern Art, New York)

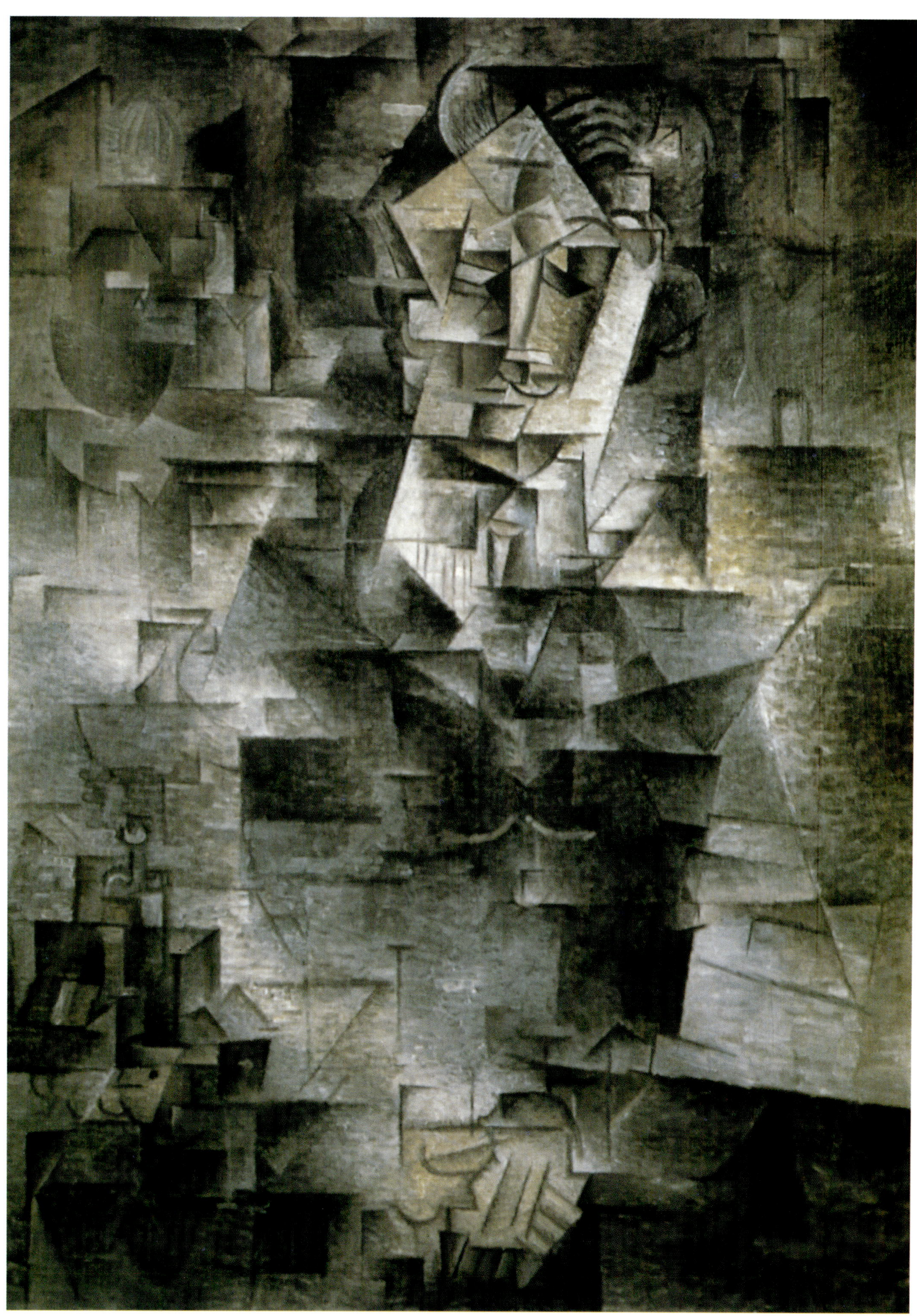

Picasso. *Portrait of D.H. Kahnweiler,* 1910
(Chicago Art Institute)

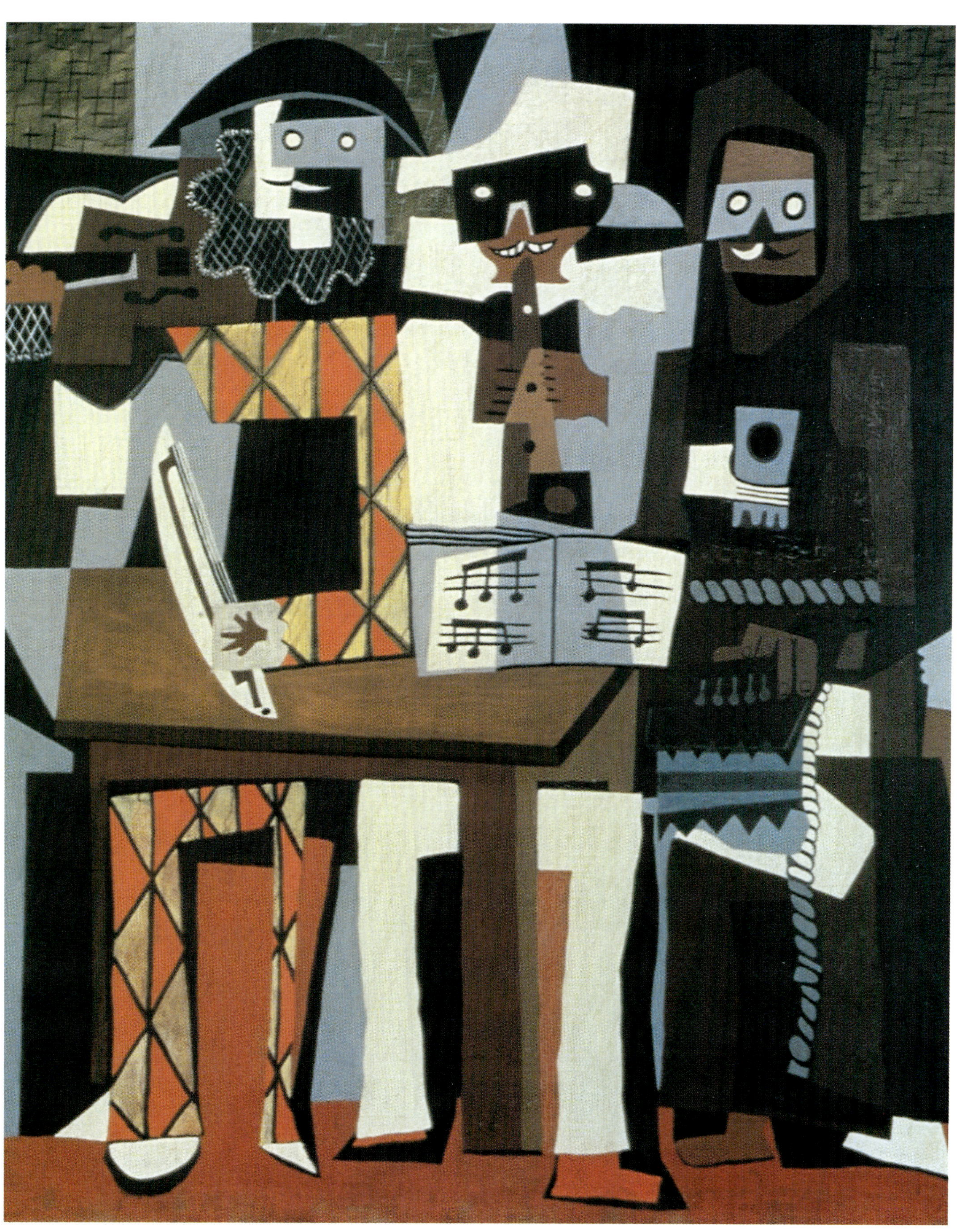

Picasso. *Three Musicians*, **1921**
(Philadelphia Museum of Art)

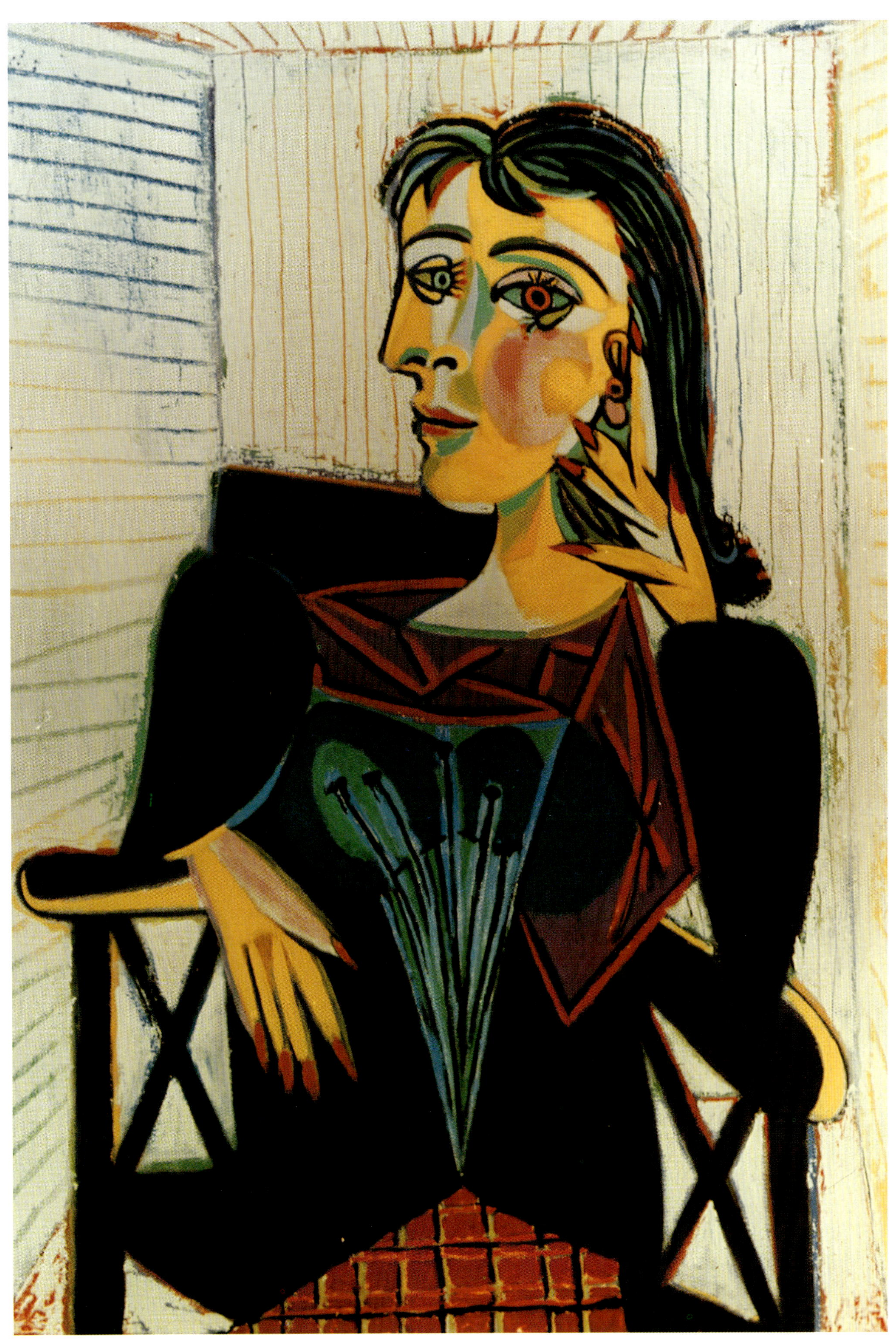

Picasso. *Portrait of Dora Maar, 1937*
(Musée Picasso, Paris)

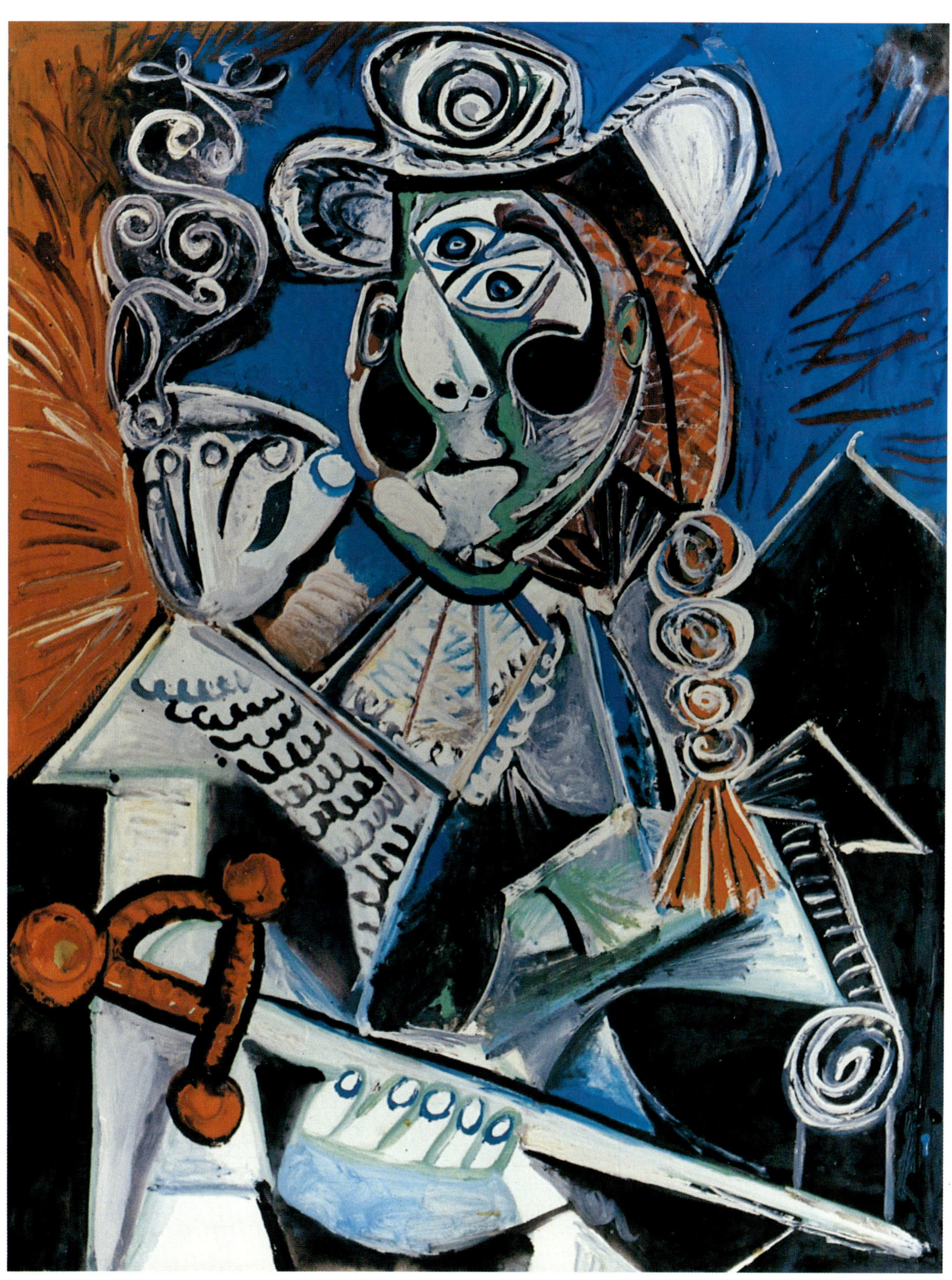

Picasso. *The Matador,* 1970
(Musée Picasso, Paris)